THE SECRETS OF THE SOUL

*An Experiential Journey
to Cosmic Reality*

Kathleen David

Copyright © 2021 by Kathleen David

All rights reserved. No part of this book may be reproduced or transmitted in any form or by any means, electronic or mechanical, including: photocopying, recording, or by any information storage and retrieval system, without permission in writing from the copyright owner.

This work is based on the experiences of an individual. Every effort has been made to ensure the accuracy of the content.

The Secrets of the Soul

An Experiential Journey to Cosmic Reality

Author: Kathleen David
Editors: Maureen Corneal, Sr. Barbaralie Stiefermann
Cover Art: Elayna Gorshenin
Interior & Cover Layout: Michael Nicloy

ISBN: (Paperback) 978-1-945907-85-2
ISBN (Hardcover): 978-1-945907-95-1

Published by
Nico 11 Publishing & Design
Mukwonago, Wisconsin
www.nico11publishing.com

Be well read.

Quantity order requests can be emailed to:
mike@nico11publishing.com

Printed in The United States of America

ARTIST STATEMENT

Within the spiritual realm, the pink lotus is the absolute of all lotus flowers. It represents divine integrity and perseverance through the inevitable difficulties of life. The yellow butterfly is seen symbolically as an emblem of transcendence and personal growth. Together, these two represent the human condition. Kathleen David poetically portrays the human condition within her book, *The Secrets of the Soul*, giving us a peek into our own essence.

Elayna Gorshenin

THE SECRETS OF THE SOUL

Dedicated to birthing the Puer
The COSMIC CHRIST within

to my daughters Siobhan, Maureen
and Erin, to my grandchildren Nahed,
Radwan and Amir, family and friends
to all nations
to the universe notwithstanding

CONTENTS

PART ONE: THE WOUNDED SOUL..7

PART TWO: THE OPENING OF LOVE...45

PART THREE: THE SECRETS OF THE SOUL ILLUMINED............71

PART FOUR: MATTERS OF THE HEART:
        A NEW BEGINNING..101

PART FIVE: THE AWAKENING HEART:
          INTELLIGENT WILL-BEING...........................139

PART SIX: THE AWAKENED HEART: INTELLIGENT ONE..........171

PART SEVEN: GOD, GIFT TO HUMANITY..191

PART EIGHT: WHAT — WHO IS THE COSMIC CHRIST?.............231

THE JOURNEY

Mother Theresa

Prayer: Take time to reflect and discover the true heart.

1. An openness of the heart.
2. Recognition of one's sinfulness and need of forgiveness.
3. Repentance: Confession and forgiveness.
4. Discern what type of life or action we are called to. Be specific.

THE PATH

The fruit of silence is prayer.

The fruit of prayer is faith.

The fruit of faith is love.

The fruit of love is service.

The fruit of service is peace.

A PSALM OF DAVID (103)

Communion prayer

Bless the Lord O my Soul and all that is within me.

Bless His holy name.

Bless the Lord O my Soul

And never forget what He has done for me.

Let my Soul be sensible of its happiness.

Let me be in the silence of all worldly cares

Taste and enjoy the sweetness of Thy presence.

It is good to hear what the Lord God will speak in me.

No one needs to be exonerated or humiliated

All needs come from within

Not without

Kathleen David

THE SECRETS OF THE SOUL

An Experiential Journey to Cosmic Reality
Dedicated to birthing the Puer, the Cosmic Christ within.

By Kathleen David

Dear Reader,

For many years I have explored the mystery of myself and the cosmos. In my search for wholeness, the thirty-six-year journey has unfolded. Perseverance, persistence and fortitude were attributes of my stubborn countenance, with light finally emerging. The search for wholeness has given way to a discovery of inner truth. The process involves a journey from fear and blind faith to faith-knowing to God-knowing to God-being. It is being in the silence in expression: activity activated, the Christ. It is my hope that this example of a living faith will encourage others to take their unique journeys thereby creating a better world for all of us.

This is a secret journey beyond space and time. While it begins with a cry and search for help from the wounded soul, it evolves into a spiraling journey of deep reverence, awe and wonder. Through meditative and contemplative prayer, the communion of soul and spirit throw light on basic truths and enhance greater understanding of the human journey, and how we are to proceed in mutuality of Thy/My will be done.

The poetic style is complemented with the descriptive passages to clarify certain characteristics and/or modes of behavior and truths. While the spiritual aspects of the book reflect the author's Catholic roots, it is embracing of all faiths and people.

No less important are the psychological experiences. The act of repentance-forgiveness, plus integration of the parts of the self: anima, animus, father (senex), mother, child (puer), shadow etc. are basic to the journey of spiritual transformation. It is equally important to note that the life drama is on-going and that the conscious birthing process continues in spiraling fashion. However, the ultimate fruits are PEACE, LOVE, JOY, HAPPINESS: those attributes intended by our loving God.

The Secrets of the Soul shows more than it tells the process of becoming whole-human and being the Presence to one another. It is a book for the person who is seriously seeking the God within. It is for the person with passionate desire to birth the true Self, that is, undergo the process of individuation. It will be of interest to those already on a similar journey, as well as the transpersonal psychologist interested in the transformational process. Because of the spiritual depth, it may be of interest to the person who is seeking new wine for new wineskins to heal the Soul.

Yours truly,
Kathleen David

PART ONE

I seek being sane in an insane world.

THE WOUNDED SOUL

I DREAM THE IMPOSSIBLE DREAM
IS IT POSSIBLE

I dream of a wholesome beautiful WORLD. I dream that You fill us so full of Your LOVE that there can be no other recourse but LOVE ABOUNDING to all the ends of the EARTH. Can You Lord Jesus answer this prayer through the power of the Holy Spirit and the wish of Your Father in heaven?

YES!

I grieve for past and present hurt, sorrow and sin. Let us rejoice in Your resurrected power and glory that brings us everlasting life. AMEN. May Your PEACE be granted in full measure to all mankind.

I dream of a beautifully ORDERED world: no hurts, no suffering and sin, no chaos, only LOVE abounding. This is my bold and brash DREAM!

SPIRIT HEART SOUL JOINED AND RECONCILED
THE MYSTERY IS SOLVED!

DESTINY

Visions in youth, dreams in old age

Chart splendorous paths in Thy Divine Plan.

Doubts and transgressions, unfulfilled goals

Disappointments, impatience and greed. Heartache and sorrows

Channeled in mystery bring Joys and Blessings and Love

Chance circumstance? Not so. Every hair counted.

Destined to become, becoming.

Moments concerns, tomorrow's delights

Actions forsaken, pleasures not taken. Heartache and sorrows

Channeled in mystery bring Joys and Blessings and Love.

Strange encounter, stranger embrace

Life's surprise and life's pleasure

Joy to the spirit; joy to the soul

Suffering dilemma, grow in the spirit. Chaos and question

Channeled in mystery bring Joys and Blessings and Love.

Order and rule, discipline and focus

Judge by the fruits:

Wisdom's fair reward.

Balance and form, charm and grace. Love and understanding

Channeled in mystery bring Joys and Blessings and Love.

GRANDVIEW

Is this God's plan in mercy? Is this God's love in blessings? Wrinkled face, bent forms, lifeless spirits helpless and dejected? Oh Life! Where is your Spirit? Oh Jeopardy! Where is your heart? Has it been hidden and buried? Has it been hurt, denied, destroyed? Come pray now. What is the Life of lives? Must not we see and feel and think and dream and hope and build a better dream?

Oh dejected spirit! Rise up and fight the battle of battles. Oh Heart! Open up and bleed and belch and vomit! Let go and let God live in the bottom-most pit of your heart so that your soul may live, and you be you forever blessed. That you be denied these favors and blessings? Oh World! I loathe you and in my torment and anguish, I fight a fight unknown to you. But listen and you shall hear and know and believe in your confusion. Sound the trumpets and fling the banners. Open the gates and herald a new reign. For you will be overpowered and mastered in a new way that only Love knows. The Kingdom will confuse and torture you. And I in my anger will fight the fight of fights to expel your greed, your ignorance. Oh that you would listen and hearken the heart and bellow of a Lover's call to resound and make all things NEW.

Oh listen My children, why torture your spirits and souls in greed and selfishness and ignorance? Open your hearts to consume and devour and choke and destroy the flames of evil so that Love and Justice and Truth and Peace can reign forever. Amen.

PRAYER OF FAITH

Oh Life! What misery. What heartache.

    My spirit tormented, broken, destroyed. Judge by the fruits.

Oh Life! Oh Jeopardy! I the Victim!

Oh Faith! That I persevere in trust and hope.

Oh Confidence! My heart made pure in body sacred to love and bear good fruit.

                Oh dare insult the 'Spirit of Grace'?

                Justice shall reign.

Oh Enlightenment! How now do I endure the contest of suffering?

    I the just woman must live by Faith.

Oh Faith! Confident in what I hope for and conviction in what I do, not see.

Oh Faith! That I be pleasing to God.

Oh Justice! That I inherit You through Faith.

Oh Obedience! I go forth not knowing where – to a foreign land of my Maker.

    So worthy of trust to receive blessings to be.

Oh Faith! Kingdoms conquered. Promises obtained. I made powerful though weak.

                Oh unworthy World! You've stripped me!

                I loathe You! Let me forgive.

Oh Perseverance! Let me run the race that lies ahead. Let me keep my eyes fixed on Jesus who inspires and perfects my faith.

Oh Endurance! Full speed ahead. Let me not abandon the struggle.

Oh Lover! My Lord, let me not disdain your discipline nor lose heart on reproof and scourging.

Oh Discipline! Let me submit to the Father and Spirits and live.

Oh Life! My Spirit, rejoice. The fruits of Peace and Justice await Thee to be healed.

Oh Victory!

PRISONER OF LOVE

I in disdain call upon Thee in my lament and seek to be wooed in Thy caress.
Oh heart, hearken and bellow. A reed blown in the wind and bent,
A swallow crippled in flight of wing. I seek comfort in Thy kiss of kisses,
And yearn for the bliss of a Lover's embrace. I am a prisoner of Love.

My heart bereft in spirit and soul; Oh that you coax me onward.
Do I forego the flesh love-call's desire to hear the heart hearken and bellow?
A reed blown in the wind and bent; a swallow crippled in flight of wing.
Hearken my lips and embrace me. I am a prisoner of Love.

Oh that You show Your love's union of flesh. I once loved in spirit and soul.
I once loved Your union of flesh; no torture of reed blown and bent in the wind,
Or swallow crippled in flight of wing. Oh God, my God! Forsake not my cry.
Hearken my lips and embrace all of me. I am a prisoner of Love.

Oh hearken lark in the meadow, your song embellish my spirit in flight.
I seek to be wooed in Thy caress. Oh trumpets blare and bugles blow.
Oh cello play and serenade me to Thy open wounded heart so sacred.
Oh to be lifted to the threshold of Thy sweet embrace.
Must I forego all earthly pleasure to be in Thy embrace? I am a prisoner of Love.

STRUGGLES ON A JOURNEY

Why Oh Lord, do You throw so much my way? How I long for moments of peace and reflection: just being—through my kitchen window, or seated in the backyard birdwatching. But now I face the rising sun, the setting sun in a business world; cruelty subtle, knocks unlimited.

Where is your peace and quiet and justice Lord? I'm too exhausted to give to a family I love so much. I'm too exhausted to clean and order a house. I'm too exhausted to spruce up a yard. All I do is give and give. Where is there a return? Where is there a resting place? Where is there a confidence and hope I struggle and carry with me each day? Your demands are so great, when can I have a day of rest? When can I have a moment of confidence, a moment of rest just for me, free of torment and feeling of loss? The losses—they go on and on: my struggles, my sorrow, my frustration, my darkness.

> Show me a glimmer of love
>
> Show me a glimmer of hope
>
> Show me a glimmer of light.

The steadfast darkness makes me weary.

> Alone I face the bleakness of gray skies
>
> Alone I face the torment of my heart and soul
>
> Alone I face the struggle of each day.

Oh endless journey, let me persevere in faith and hope and trust and seek

> A new tomorrow
>
> A new dawn
>
> A new day
>
> A new hope

A new love

A new faith

A new trust

A new confidence

A new light

A new justice

A new You, Lord God Father Almighty.

Let my shattered spirit in a shattered body rise up and fight a new fight to persevere in hope for Your coming, Your presence, Your enlightenment, Your wisdom, Your strength, Your power, Your Glory! Amen.

TRIUMPH OF LOVE

Let me hear the Word of the Lord. What is your grievance against me Lord? My lack of faithfulness, my lack of mercy, my lack of knowledge of you and your way? Bad fruit follows bad fruit. I mourn that which surrounds me is in sadness. Nothing lives. Nothing is alive!

Yes, I ignored Your law, my Lord. I've sinned against You in my disdain. I am punished for my ways and deeds. I eat but am not satisfied. I abandoned You my Lord, I the guilty. I have forsaken my God. I did not listen. But God's love endures forever. The trial foreshadows my wholehearted return to my Maker, Whose love endures me forever.

SEARCH OF A LONELY HEART

Alone at dawn's awakening call; alone in prayer and coffee time.

Alone in readiness for world affairs, captivated, engrossed in day's events.

Alone again at evening tide, dusk enveloping, dark at last, alone and lonesome heart.

Nature's store: incomplete yearning of a lover's love for companion/friend,

Quiet reflection lost in hope and desire, deep secrets and wishes aired,

Humble directness and openness shared. What price! What mystery!

Does destiny rule? Dark mystery. Alone and lonesome hearth.

Submission following struggles and despair: question, search, bewilderment,

Watchful hope followed by hope. Can I have love of my desire, or am I destined

To be not of my choice but design? Can I hope or shall I forget?

What painful choice for a Lover to make. God direct my impoverished Soul.

Oh question directed to my heart. Oh search implanted in my Soul. Oh Quandary!

Perhaps an answer You hold firm. Awaken and direct me quickly.

Let not my heart perish in the flames.

Light up my life with new news. Awaken my heart and let my spirit be alive.

Hold my hand and lead me to Thy threshold. Direct my ways and my heart's desires.

Lead me to fertile fields and rich rewards. Awaken my soul!

Grant me new garments for my spirit, refurbished in gold and splendorous array.

Oh yearning heart, impoverished spirit, my sleeping soul awaits.

Surely Thy bounty awaits Thee. Spirit, come alive! Heart, be strengthened!

Sustain my mercurial soul. Dark road, lighten. Where is the path,

Obliviated in torment and distress? No rest or comfort until Thy Firmness You implant.

Clarify! Make known Thy way for me. Hold me not in bondage.

Subservient to Thy way I await Thy response to loving, hoping, and questioning,

To seek sleep and awake refreshed: Heart Spirit and Soul made NEW!

MY HAVEN AND MY HOME

Oh Lord, Protector of my strength and courage

Your child wanders in the city of decay. Deliver me from evil

And protect me from the wiles of deceitful acts and torment of false speech.

For You Lord are my Haven and my Home.

My cries are heard in the bleak winter.

Even though the Shadows confuse me, and the paths are dark,

Faith is my armor and Trust is my staff.

For You Lord are my Haven and my Home.

In cloistered array, my spirit rejoices in small favors.

My soul is embellished like the spread of angel wings.

My heart is protected and comforted in the midst of all evil.

For You Lord are my Haven and my Home.

TWO LOVES

Two Loves treasure One. One must let go; the other becomes rooted and grows.

Go forth Loser! Find new grounds.

I'm the loser. Where shall I go? Where shall I wander?

Or do I wait for Heaven's Gate?

Two Loves treasure One. Not workable; I shall flee in pain.

But in my ship, I shall chart a new course, though my desires deny such.
Meet me new Love. Show me Your face. Grant me new hope.
I'm lost in tears and pain.

The road is weary; plagued and confused too long. Stop for refreshment.
Oh Heart! Break not in pain and doubt. Fortitude will see you through.
Open Heart, watchful and on guard, if Wisdom shows you another course,
You shall know no fear or doubt. Trust and Faith will steer you clear.

JOURNEY HOME

Oh lonely lonesome yearning Heart
Shattered torn fragmented plagued split uprooted rejected blamed
Tortured brazened stabbed destroyed. Oh lonesome Heart!
Shout and cry! Free your Soul to Victory.

Oh lonely lonesome yearning Heart
Scattered seed in raging winds, sunken vessel in turbulent seas
Vehement, all powerful pervasive force. Heart be opened!
Choose to love. Free your Soul to Victory.

Oh lonely lonesome yearning Heart
Comfort be your ransomed gift; succumb to a Lover's love for you.
Embellished spirit Thy reward, wholesome tender gentle Love
Your Soul victorious, freed at last to journey Home.

ODE TO A LOST LOVE

I am drunk with wine. Oh Lord, heal me in Your splendor.

You have stripped me of my heart's desire and longing.

You have taken away the fabric of my life.

I am faltering. I know not Your secret way.

Let me find a resting place, an abode of comfort.

Heal and deliver me from my obstinacy. Let this pain be welcomed now,

But not accepted guest for long, for fear of grief in dead repose,

Destructive raging horror; perhaps to cease, and then destroy upon return.

Help me to anticipate anew.

Let my tears be special, cleansing and releasing me of wounds.

Heal my hurts and loss, Oh Lord. I loved too much in short a time.

Heal my hurts and loss.

I am drunk with wine. Oh Lord, heal me in Your splendor.

Infirmities have pounced like wolves on prey;

Love before its own time I pursued. Heal me Oh Lord of my infirmities.

How could I be deprived of loving so great a Love as You? I have found Your secret way.

NO LONGER DILLYDALLY ON WHAT COULD HAVE BEEN

What could have been was full and sweet

What could have been was precious and delicate

What could have been was God filled and beloved

What could have been, ever deemed holy and blessed.

What is, is harsh reality

What is, is facing disappointment and failure

What is, is falling down and getting up again

What is, is broken heart and broken spirit.

What needs to be is rising up again.

What needs to be is hope and perseverance.

What needs to be is healing love for self, sheer indulgence.

Too stripped to go on in vain? Indulge Thyself; rest and heal.

Patiently does Thy Love reciprocate. Lovingly does Thy Love embrace.

Joyfully does Thy Love imbue rich gained freedom in Thy path.

Dreadful ego stripped of fault,

New enlightened heart upholds while lofty heights await Thee.

CHANGE

Change, let me welcome you beyond the threshold of my doorstep. Come in and join me for a spell. In your stripping, I will delight in new adventures. Though saddened, I will rejoice. Right now, I'm so unsure; on sandy soil I walk. Where are you taking me? Comfort me on the way. I'm not afraid, but I'm so puzzled, and I don't know where I'm going. The path is dark and mysterious. Perhaps I seek to travel too fast. The journey must be well paced and timed. I need the wisdom to slow down and let the storms be cleared. The sun will shine upon my path and light each step.

Change! Welcome! Step beyond my threshold. I will dance to your rhythms of the unknown.

BLESSED BE WE POOR IN SPIRIT

Glorious is Your reign. Magnificent in all Your splendor. Victorious in mission. We give thanks.

> Blessed be we poor in spirit: FAITH our armor.
>
> Darkness
>
> Helplessness
>
> Striving
>
> Mercy
>
> Forgiveness
>
>
> Deliver us Oh Lord. We give thanks.
>
> Question
>
> Doubt
>
> Fear

> Anger
>
> Resentment
>
> Hurt
>
> Lack of acceptance
>
> Guilt

Blessed be we poor in spirit: HOPE our armor.

> Glimmer of light
>
> Sufficiency
>
> Achievement
>
> Love
>
> Recompense

PEACE: A goal to be strived for. We give thanks.

Blessed be we poor in spirit: LOVE our armor.

> Light
>
> Grace
>
> Perseverance
>
> Enlightenment
>
> Obedience
>
> Endurance
>
> Discipline

We give thanks.

    Resolution

    Certainty

    Acceptance

    Peace

    Justice

    Truth

Glorious is Your reign. Magnificent in all Your splendor. Victorious in mission. We give thanks.

THIS IS THE DAY

This is the day to start anew. This is the day to boldly rise.

This is the day to see with open eyes, and count the blessings of my life.

This is the day that truth abounds, rich and mellow as old wine.

This is the day of yearning's blossom: full fruition of joy in life.

PRAISE TO YOU LORD SHEPHERD

Praise to You Lord Shepherd of good will Who grants me peace.

Praise to You Lord Shepherd Who guards me from evil.

Praise to You Lord Shepherd Who guides my footsteps in dark passages.

Praise to You Lord Shepherd Who comforts me in my need.

Praise to You Lord Shepherd.

SECRET JOURNEY

I want to steer our ship from perils of the deep and dark, God willing,

Blast through space and time to reach a dream unknown to most mankind.

In space we blast the rocket ship beyond the realms of earth to meet the dawn

Of Heaven's Gate to build a Kingdom, not small but great.

You, small child in love; I mad, bold with daring love will steer the ship.

You, special gift with favor blessed whose companion's light you be.

You are so powerful; you are so strong. You are a fighter all the way.

But strange, I am the pilot now, and you the dimmer light.

On perilous journey we proceed, a challenge to our hearts.

Oh glimmering light! Shine on! Shine on! We'll meet the dawn

Of Heaven's Gate to build a Kingdom, not small but great.

Oh blinding light! Oh piercing beam! Your power and strength anew.

You are a fighter all the way. Not so strange. You're pilot now,

And you the blinding light. Now you want to steer our ship

From perils of the deep and dark, God willing,

Blast through space and time to reach a dream unknown to most mankind.

THE NARROW ROAD

Will you take me on this journey alluring and adventurous?

Will you take me on this journey dark and rough?

Will you take me on this journey perilous and frightening?

Will you take me on this journey where love abounds?

Will you take me on this journey in the presence of my peers?

                    What will we seek? What will we find?

We'll seek treasures known only to our heart.

We'll seek light-filled lamps to direct us.

We'll seek wisdom to shelter us and comfort us in the storm.

We'll seek justice and holiness born of truth.

I will take you on this journey alluring and adventurous.

I will take you on this journey dark and rough.

I will take you on this journey perilous and frightening.

I will take you on this journey where love abounds.

I will take you on this journey in the presence of your peers.

                    What will you seek? What will you find?

You'll seek protection from confused and evil men.

You'll seek love for your enemy and reprimand him with kindness and love.

You'll seek discipline and fortitude in the presence of indulgence and worldly cares.

You'll seek life built on a rock that bears good fruit.

You'll seek to be a lamb among wolves: clever as a serpent but innocent as a dove.

Let us come with you on this journey alluring and adventurous.

Let us come with you on this journey dark and rough.

Let us come with you on this journey perilous and frightening.

Let us come with you on this journey where love abounds.

Let us come with you on this journey in the presence of our peers.

What will we seek? What will we find?

We'll seek to be nothing to discover who we are.

We'll seek to be open to the spirit speaking through us.

We'll seek to be persevering and steadfast in the time of trial.

We'll seek to be with Jesus and gather with Him.

We'll seek peace in all ways.

FORGIVING LOVE

Oh Fear, Resentment, Hate, let go! Oh Anger, Frustration, let go!

Heal! Be well. God's love will shelter Thee and protect Thee.

Forgive. How difficult a task. Oh burdensome Your demand.

Forgive. Let go and Love!

DEATH AND RESURRECTION

The stillness of night encroaches; laden tasks left incomplete.

The dawn of tomorrow beckons, wherewith my death and resurrection.

Oh challenge of my heart! My soul deep buried in grief.

The gift of love pervades all seasons and brings hope to my death.

The shadows are bold and unflinching; the task at hand near spent.

I've failed again and try to see the Love in failure.

RESIGNATION

The choice is made. The cards have been played. Let Thy heart not resist the stakes at hand. No more questions or decision, though sadness looms. Heart's broken store will forgive, but not forget.

Break away Heart, Mind and Soul! Break away! Be strong! Free YOU of torment and pain. Spirit! Spring joyfully forth. New pastures await Thee, rich lush and green. Oh Sadness! Joy replace Thee. Embellished Spirit and Soul, rise up! All is not in vain. Let go of anger, resentment and frustration.

Your destiny speaks plainly. No more confusion! Let go. Love Thyself! The past has fruits of no avail. Move on and hope for gain. Love's store and Love's reward will step forth. Have faith and persevere. Weariness and oppression have swept Thee far out into the tide. Come back to dry ground and walk erect.

No longer torn, blown and rent by stormy waves; solid, steadfast and firm is the ground beneath. No longer bewildered, confused or lost; clear and direct, firmly are planted Thy footsteps. Heal and be well. Give up heartache, sorrow and loss.

Receive joy and happiness. The decision is made for Thee. Struggle not with the shadows of the past. Hope! Thy soul's beacon light, shine forth! Dispel the darkness! Blot out the tears. Clear the path for rays of sunshine. Old sins are forgiven with no regrets. A new account is opened by Thy Soul's light. Shiny bright and crystal clear is Thy path of hope.

Grow, divine spark within and explode Thy whole great Universe! May all the creative forces lead, direct and strengthen Thee. A new tomorrow awaits Thee.

LOSING

Life is truly a series of continuous losses:

>Each loss expresses gain
>
>Each hope expresses pain
>
>Each desire expresses fantasy
>
>Each reality expresses grief
>
>Each truth expresses wisdom
>
>Each dream expresses yearning
>
>Each heartache expresses sorrow
>
>Each sorrow expresses creative losing (gain).

Must I go on to explain the dream of dreams – the yearning of the SOUL?

RESTORATION

Bruised and scratched from barbs of life, Golden Lion look at me.

Compassionate, loving, sorrowful eyes; share your gentle company.

Come to me quickly; rescue me from my enemies.

Blot out the tears and wipe away the tears.

Stroke my cheek and fill my cup with vintage wine.

Darken not the light of day. Shine the ruby stars ablaze. Glisten,

Even in the dimmest light, cloudburst rainbows over yon horizon bright.

Golden Lion, comfort me the lamb in need.

Delicate as baby's breath, intricate as Irish lace,

Fragile as the snowflake fallen, restore me to the joy of LIFE.

THE SEARCH FOR WISDOM

Seek and search for wisdom My people, for Wisdom is the key to our protection:

Our safety from destructions man made

        nuclear/chemical arms to destroy all of us

        ruthless devastation of Mother Earth

        inner despair (a lack of hope).

Let our leaders be stable and calm.

Teach and instruct us Oh Solomon.

    Let us take heed of your way and seek prudence.

    Let us plead so Wisdom may come to us as to you.

    Let us prefer Her to riches and wealth and prestige.

    Beyond all measure let us love and seek and cherish Her.

    Even beyond light, let us recognize and seek and invite Her.

    No doubt all else will want to be in Her company.

For Wisdom is Mother and rules

    Let us rejoice in Her: this secret treasure timeless.

    And recognize that God is sole director in thought and word and deed.

For in little things:

> nature's laws and nature's habits
>
> creature's ways and thought and creature's actions

Both secret hidden, and open and direct.

Wisdom, Mother of all is teacher and leader and instructor.

For Mother so pure:

She pervades all existence, all life, all being.

She so beautiful, so fragile, so sensitive, so loving

The expression of

> all that is wise
>
> all that is good
>
> all that is pure
>
> all that is powerful.

For She speaks of God in His magnificent glory here on earth.

How can such be described that is so divine:

> fairer than fair
>
> powerful in her rule
>
> just in all fruits.

I seek Her in my blunderings and crippled wounds of humanity.

I see Her in my pain and hurt and loss and anger and frustrations.

Would that I benefit from such yearning desire and love and longing.

For from Her splendor I will learn of Her prudence in service;

Of Her fruits in all their splendor and richness.

For Wisdom so pure and holy and free and unblemished

So filled with love and peace

Far greater than the constellations, the stars, the moon, the planets.

Let us taste the renewal of all things through Her divine expression.

Let us seek Her as friends and rulers and prophets for God's Kingdom.

Let us seek Her for the riches and beauty She offers and bestows with abundance.

Let us seek Her for instruction in all virtues:

> Prudence, Justice, Fortitude
>
> Counselor while all is well
>
> Comforter in sorrow and grief.

For Judgment is keen even in youth, and listeners take heed in awe.

Life with Her bears not grief but gladness of heart and Joy.

Oh Immortal Wisdom

> Be my light, my companion, my guide and director of cosmic and minute, of small and large, little and big.
>
> Be my Lover in the midst of all elements.

LIFE HAS TAUGHT ME MANY THINGS

Life has taught me many things

> To walk and to speak and to survive
>
> To hide and to blot out the real me
>
> To forego and forget; To be less than whole
>
> To be warped and afraid to be bold.

Life has retaught me through hard knocks

> Oh harsh reality, can your vehement lash abate
>
> Oh perseverance, can you go on and on

Oh patience, can you survive?

Shed the guilt. Become whole. Love sustaineth Thee.

Life has taught me many things

Enemies in disguise seek to devour and destroy

Do not condone the wide road of false friends

Do not try to change what you cannot control

Do not waste energies on closed hearts and ears.

Life has taught me many things

That order and rule are godly

To pray that I be delivered from confused and evil men

To be strengthened in faith and in trials

That I've been protected and blessed amidst my sin, chaos and defeat.

Life has taught me many things

The power of prayer

The test of true friendship

The Love of God: His protection, care and power

That gifts, wisdom and talents do reside providing I comply.

Yes! Life has taught me many things

The Love of God

The Love in Joy

The Love in the Golden Rule

Happiness can be real.

TAKE TIME TO SMELL THE ROSES

Enjoy each moment of your day

Indulge in beauties of your place

See the brightness of the light

Hear the sounds of all your life

Touch your loved ones with your warmth

Feel the presence of Thy power

Taste the joys of honeyed fruit

Tell – speak the truth in all Thy ways

Awaken in me the breath of life-giving strength.

ODE TO JOY

Refrain: Joy! Joy! Joy!

What mystery of life

An impossible dream made real

Praise, thanks and glory to our Maker.

Joy! Joy! Joy!

My heart is filled with joy

I need freedom and you need freedom

So together we can build not what we see or think.

Joy! Joy! Joy!

We persevere in trust and hope, the building of a dream

Not clear, but real. Not tangible, not fathomable

But together we can build not what we see or think.

Joy! Joy! Joy!

Love rules and conquers

In justice we'll proclaim a new dawn, a new day, a Kingdom

We'll build on rock a solid base, not what we see or think.

Joy! Joy! Joy!

Blessed be this day. A love so great, a task so real

A vision robed in splendor, Reality deemed blessed.

In hope and trust and confidence, a Kingdom ever blessed.

Joy! Joy! Joy!

A vision we extol

We are so powerful. We are so strong and forceful

The puzzle pieces fit. We're builders, not what we see or think.

Joy! Joy! Joy!

Shall I disclose the mystery?

A glorious Kingdom. Not tangible, not fathomable

But together we can build not what we see or think.

LIVING WATERS

In the valley of Peace we met, my Jesus and I

In the valley of Living Waters I wandered into the arms of my Beloved

In the quiet peace of dim lit walls I bowed my head

And behold, His healing Love descended upon me and broke the silence.

In sorrowful reparation; in faith and trust

In petition, song, praise and thanksgiving

Each healed according to his/her need

Peace ever-present. Joyous Love abounding.

WALK GENTLY MY LOVE

Walk gently, My Love in the eve of Life

Your footsteps soft-treading in the dim moonlight.

Our shadows bask in the dampness

And stark-naked is the revealing eye

To strip bare the branches of my loved one.

Oh Come! My Love, take my hand

And I will lead you to the newness of life.

Blot your tears and let go of fears

The dance to the unknown rhythm is about to begin.

Follow in my footsteps. Soon you will not need your guide.

Walk gently, My Love in the eve of Life

Of boldness and beauty you are enthralled.

The loss of early dawn of Life is here

Accept your newness to Be and Become

And go beyond the barren gate.

Walk gently, My Love in the eve of Life

You are a special gift. Oh Life's Mystery!

Thwart not the path. Reveal and make new Love's way.

Renew the heart and embellish the spirit

The broken wounds are immersed in Life!

Let us be transformed in the eve of Life

And journey in the presence of love and light.

BE BECOMING WHOLE

Today beckons. Tomorrow calls

Love's sight is amply restored

Enveloping my Being with healing Power

Rest in comfort and in peace

Granted these favored gifts to Thee in life's mystery.

Be Becoming Whole

Gone are deep hurts: pain released

Freed from endless hours of work and pain

Road to self-discovery pursued: Mystery unveiled, unknown
Now, discover who you are.

BE STILL AND LOVE

Be still and listen. In the twilight hour take rest.
Retreat to the chambers of the heart in search of mystery.
Thine own Self come forth and shout the cry of Victory.
Be opened!
Walk in the desert path until you reach spring waters
And quench your thirst.
The dry parched waste renewed with waters overflowing
Will calm your hearts and give peace.
Be still and love.

THE WAYFARER: Ode to Father Joe

A Rock
Not idol
But human, whole example
Sinner and Saint
Shepherd

A Rock
Steadfast Whole Tough
A laugh, a sigh, a tear brushed gently

Joyous outburst

Welcome Heart

Unflustered in worldly torment

Embellished spirit

God's gift in love and mercy.

A Rock

Stooped form

Sometimes fatigued

Saddened Stressed

Competent Compassionate Committed

Lighthearted

Friend in need

God's gift in love and mercy.

A Rock

Generous Kind

Direct Sincere Honest

Unshakable in Faith

Simple Profound

Cautious Wise in counsel

Authoritative Comforter

God's gift in love and mercy.

A Rock

Comrade

Playmate Friend

Humorous encounter

Party Giver

Joy filled laughter and fun

Spirit of Christmas

God's gift in love and mercy.

A Rock

Not idol

But human, whole example

Sinner and Saint

Shepherd

A Rock

Fortitude your Strength

Truth your Light

Discipline with Prudence your Rod

Justice your Robe

Mother Wisdom your Staff

Love your Crown

God's gift in love and mercy.

KNOWLEDGE OF YOUR WILL

My goal and object is to seek the knowledge of Your will

    to be the best I can be

    to build the Kingdom of God on earth and realize it

    to see it happening around me in the world

    to see suffering, pain, hurt and brokenness transformed into joy and peace of the Kingdom

    to see an abiding love and happiness free of violence and sin for all the earth

    to see the Kingdom of God fully manifested on earth as well as in heaven freeing God's people from poverty and hunger.

This is my dream.

CONVERSION

How can sorrow and a sad heart be turned into Joy?

    The mysteries of life sober and perplex us

    The wellspring of joy come from abandonment

    The soul thirst

    The mind tricks us

    The heart is swayed

    We are so vulnerable to good and evil

    Out of humble awakenings we are opened

    And made so helpless, the Pursued

    The Victim of God's Love.

WISDOM OF THE FOOL

If I can learn to seek nothing but You, then I will be free and no longer grieve the present/past/future losses in my life. You expect so much my Lord. When in time and space will You receive the desires and wishes of my heart?

Am I a fool or You, or both of us fools? Fools rush in! Yes, I am a fool. Wise men never fall in love. But then, where does Wisdom play the role of countess, king or knave? Or is Wisdom all of these in many roles and plays? Perplexed, astounded, angered, resentful, confused, I come to You. I challenge You to love and show Your face and grant Your love to me: a fool who wishes to love and be loved. Grant me Your favored blessing. Amen.

COMMUNION OF SPIRIT AND SOUL

Spirit

    Sing to me my Love

    Dance to a gypsy bandolier

    Shout to the sun beaten limbs of broken stone hearts

    Bring a feast of lamb and juniper

    Tapered vessels with robust burgundy

    To toast Love's triumphant victory.

Soul

    Pears and lace grace my body

    Sweet violets permeate the air

    Lips, smooth and full are pink

    To match the glow of amber skin.

Spirit

    Sing to me my Love

    Bring me fresh flowers that bloom by the roadside

    Bring me a basket of wild roses and honeysuckle

    I'm a wild rambling flower of Life

    Dancing as the dandelion carried by the wind

    Free and untainted by the world.

Soul

    Stretch out your arms to greet me

    Let my kisses refresh your memory

    The scent of apple clusters ripening in your garden lure me to your chamber

    Let not my heart be stirred to love before its appointed time.

Spirit

    Your sail beaten face shows your bold and beautiful countenance

    Come to my garden where the air is perfumed with lilies, pine and geranium

    Sage and mint spice the air

    The violets and honeysuckle stir memories of our first greeting

    Take my hand and I will lead you

    To the spring waters to quench our thirst.

Soul

    The journey has been labored with uncertainty

    Your garden is a haven for my weary body

    I'll rest and be still until morning

    Then we'll climb the crescent to behold the noonday sun.

Spirit

    The spring's water will cool and refresh us

    We'll feast on berries and mountain trout

    And walk the narrow path until dusk

    The plaintive call of the whippoorwill's song will remind us not to linger

    For the day is gone

    And we must go.

Soul

    My heart has been stirred to love you

    Your smile and light-filled eyes

    Arouse my desire to hold you close

    Forever.

PART TWO

The angel of sorrow is the Angel of Deliverance
Michael the Archangel restores.

THE OPENING OF LOVE

PRAYER OF THANKS AND SUPPLICATION

I am healed and whole NOW.

Thank You Thank You Thank You God.

Come little children. Come one and all.

Fill us with wholeness.

Fill us with light.

Fill us with wisdom.

Lord, help me to see the God in all things.

Lord, help me to see the God of mercy.

Lord, help me to see the God in all men/women.

Lord, help me to see the God in evil.

Make a plea for holiness.

Lord, grant me the gift/grace of holiness.

Help me to love You with all my heart, my soul, my mind, my strength.

Help me to love my neighbor as myself.

STATEMENT OF BEING

MOTHER   of holiness

of wholeness

of oldness

FATHER   of holiness

of wholeness

of the loathing of evil

of the hole in our hearts

of evil

of eros

Make us whole

Thou makest evil whole

Thou makest eros whole

Thou makest the worldly whole

Thou makest the blind see

Thou makest the deaf and dumb see

Thou makest the birthing of Me.

You are the soul of liberty

You are the servant of the simple way

You are the servant of Me me

You are the servant of the evening

You are the servant of the morning

You are the servant of all humanity

You are the servant in me

You are the servant of oldness

You are the servant of birthing

You are the servant of longing

You are the servant of living a whole/holy life

You are the servant of loving

You are the servant of perfect one

You are the servant of mercy

You are the servant of sanctity

You are the servant of healing

You are the servant of mystery

You are the servant/soul of the love of evil. AMEN!

NOVENA TO THE DARKNESS OF THE EARTH

Deliver us from loathing the home of our sanctity.

Deliver us from loathing the sins of our home.

Deliver us from loathing the secrets of the sons of evil.

Deliver us from loathing the secrets of our hearts.

Deliver us from loathing the home of Eros.

Deliver us from loathing the Sons of God for seeking the forgiveness of the sin of pride.

Deliver us from loathing Eros, for Mary's and Joseph's hiding the Christ-child.

Free us. Free us.

Free us. Free us.

You have seen the hope of the World (Angel of Hope)!

The Son/Sun will clothe the body in light
And all evil/disease will be consumed.

The night of the Soul is mothering the Satan: the Sorrow.

The Glory of God is the angel of light.

Eros of old is the Satan (unwhole).

DELIVERANCE

Lord, thank You for delivering us from loathing our sacred side. You are the Mother of Hope for the new way. Our way is wholesome. Michael the Archangel is wholesome, born in the spirit of wholeness. You/I are the spirit of the first born of Eros. You/I are the Soul of Dabar in ME. Mary and Joseph are born of Abraham. Mary and Joseph are Sons of Dabar who picked the Son/Soul of Jesus. Through Michael is the love of the Spirit of ME. You are the sin of me transformed. You have the grace of losing me in the Sacred. You are the Savior of the Soul.

Deliver us from evil in Eros and Dabar in the Soul of mystery.

HEALING AND DELIVERANCE IN THE SORROW OF EVIL

Heal us Oh Lord.

Heal us in the SOUL.

Heal us Oh Lord.

Heal us in the SOUL of the secret of mystery.

Heal us Oh Lord in mystery.

Heal us to see in the SOUL of me.

Help me to see the hope/home of deliverance of Thy mission for us.

Give us the secret healing.

Give us the secret of healing our SOUL: THAT OUR SECRET SIDE WILL LOVE OUR SOUL.

Help me to see the Savior of the living LIBERTY.

Help us to right the sign of LOVE.

Help us to right the sins of the HOME.

Thank You for the deliverance of my SOUL from evil longing.

Your mercy is the secret hope of the deliverance of Eros, of Dabar of
SOULS NOW IN THE SORROW OF EVIL.

Mary and Joseph are the simple WAY.

I have the heart of loving the simple WAY.

Jesus has found you.

Jesus has fed you.

Jesus enfolds you.

Jesus has fed us the light of the deliverance from evil.

Jesus has offered a sign of me.

Mary and Joseph heal the poorest souls in love and life.

Heal us in the soul of sorrow.

Heal us in the soul of sinfulness.

Deliver us from evil in the secrets of the SOUL.

Deliver us from evil in the secrets of the sins of the world.

Save us from the SOUL of the sins of me.

Mother, Father of Jesus, hear me NOW!

Go to the Soul of Jesus.

Jesus is in the labor of the SOUL.

Hear the SOUL of ME.

Deliver us from the evil of longing.

Christ, the Kingdom is here.

Heal the SOUL of the eye of anger.

Heal the SOUL of the eye of sorrow.

FATHER OF LIGHT MOTHER OF LOVE

Father of Light, Mother of Love

Teach us to be holy for the Liberty of the SOUL

For Home, Service and LOVE.

Eros knows the love required for ordered service.

Mary and Joseph know too.

Mary and Joseph are in the HEART.

Eros is in the SOUL.

Motherhood of LOVE

Teach us to be a seal of HOPE.

Heal the cross of me.

You know the SOUL of my Father.

You are a channel of LOVE.

You are a channel of HOPE.

You are a channel of MOTHERHOOD.

Eros knows.

Thank You Thank You GOD.

OUR FATHER

Our Father of LIFE

Help me to seek the home of Eros

In all of me.

Our Father Who art in hell

Help me build the understanding of the seed

With help of sinners.

Eros of evil

Help us live a bountiful way.

The bountiful way is the secret of evil

Of sight of me.

RELATIONSHIP

ME – My Divine Self Speaks

Bless me Father.

I have sinner/errored.

I thank You for Your constant forgiving Love.

I have gotten lost.

Show Me the way home.

Relationship.

    Oneness.

    Interdependence.

OUR FATHER WHO ART ME

Our Father Who art ME

Hallowed is my home – LOVE

My kingdom come

My will be done on earth

As it is in heaven

Give us this day our daily bread

As we forgive those who trespass

Against us and lead.

Our Father Who art alive

In the Spirit of ME

Hallowed be the RULE.

Our Father

Son of God Son of Man Eros

Our Father of light Who art ME

Our Father Who lives in me now

Wholly proclaim with passion and

Fill us with the Love of Jesus

For wholeness, for righteousness

For home, for poor, for the son of David

My Son of day.

You are the home of Eros of me

The secret of sorrow of me

The Father of pride

I and the Father are soul in the home.

Our Father

Who art in the lips

Go forth. Proclaim the Soul is healing.

You are a seeker of loving the soul I have now.

Our Father Who art in Earth

Our Father Who art alive in me

Hallowed by Thy Name

Thy Kingdom is here

Thy will is being done

On earth as it is in heaven

You give us this day our daily bread

And forgive us our trespasses

As we forgive those who trespass against us

And lead us.

Our Father

Who art the living ME

Hallowed by my home

I am the divine light empowered

Behold the Son of God.

Our Father Who art giving me
Hallowed be me
You live one ME!

Our Father
Who has delivered us home
The light shine upon us
The light be with us
Pray for us
Lead us home.

Our Father
Who art in home with us
Father, You are alone with ME now.
No one wants to be alone with moral man
One wants to be alone with the SOUL
Your Father is One with the SOUL.

Our Father Who art ME
Ever present
Hallowed be Thee/ME
Thy/My will be done
On Earth as it is in Thee

Let us be the Bread of Life

Now and forever.

Amen.

Thank You God

So be it

Thy Love Thy Majesty

Thy might and power

Ever glorious

Unto Thee/ME.

Our Father

Holy is/are us

Whole of home

Hear us alone in the silence

Hear us alone in the home

Hear us alone in the Son/Sun of old

Hear us

Hear me alone

Every heart of even tells the Soul

The heel/heal of lies

Join the Soul of ME

I am the Soul of even/evil of old

Give a home in me.

Our Father Who are ME

Whenst have I fallen to such a state

Separate from Thou Who art my Life, my Bread?

I return to You my shelter and abode

For compensation of long forgotten past

Redeem my ways, my discontent to Be my Beloved Evermore.

Have I not been strong enough in Christ's strength Who strengthens me
To persevere in patience and follow Thy welcomed bliss made manifold
Through me, with me and in me?

Return not an eye for an eye Oh Beloved full of awe and grace.
Shelter Thy weaknesses in the strength of Thy Maker. Evermore. Amen.

MYSTERY OF DESIRE

I am My Self and me obliterated by the sea of Divine Light

Oh Come to me I beckon

Thine own desire and will beseech Thee

Make haste. In ME is blessed GRACE

Tumult expanded spent

I am Thine own Power bestowed!

The Soul yearns for God expression

This day I wander in the deep

To behold the mystery of desire.

SOLITUDE

Solitude

Not mine But Thine

Henceforth

Thy/My will be done

Seek Sought Found

Let the ashes pile up

Smoldering flames

Gone out

Dissipated

Grace granted

In Our solitude

Thank You God

Volatile

Vulnerable

Volcanic – spew over

Seek not vain pleasure

BE
LOVE
DO

THE HOUSE
Don't worry!
I abide in Thee
Thou in ME
Holy is Thy Sepulcher
Make straight Thy Way
Holy is Thy Name

Behold the Son of God

BE PRESENT NOW

Leaves fallen, amber rust

A little more sadness dissipated

Gloom trods at my back door; open the front (door).

Let the sun shine in. The moment is gone.

Be now, ever present to the Glorious Resurrection. Amen.

THE WORD

I am the Word too divinely expressed in symbols not so clear.

Ponder child, and you shall see heaven's sent gift to Thy/My people.

Oh bliss! Live on! Grace granted, bestowed. Amen.

TRUST

Oh Universe, I embrace You/Thee. Jerusalem, struggle no more.

Give up the fight. Be.

I peacefully encounter the soul, well and whole.

My spirit grants the soul rest and healing. Nurture Thyself.

Grow and bloom. Welcome spring, My beloved child. Endure the winter harvest.

Tis short. Trust My/Thy self. Amen.

SOUL'S JOURNEY

Remembrance, long forgotten boldly emanates in tranquil waters.

Stark simplicity. Utter chaos gone, dissipated.

Love's embellishment blossoms forth. No longer hindered, trust ensues.

I am at one with You/Thee in peace. Amen.

BELIEF ENDEARMENT NOBLE BLESSINGS

How blessed is Thy light, Oh Son/Sun. Bring forth Thy healing touch

So blinded man may see the good in all that is and Be.

Spring forth dear child anew. Adventure, keen and full of love.

Expectancy befits a King/Queen.

Oh Wise One, I beseech Thee to love and be and do. I AM. I AM You!

YOU KNOW THAT I KNOW

I am

You am

We am

They am

He am

She am

It am

All of us AM

MISSION REQUIRES

Integrity	Glory
Readiness	Substance
Ability	Rule
Force	Order
Purpose	Seasoning
Love	Laughter
Honor	Play
Obedience	Dreams

THE MYSTICAL MOMENT

Thank You God for Your bounty

My heart wells up in Joy

The Mystical Moment

Blessed Grace

Unencumbered

Peace

Love take hold

Sharing

Communion

Balance

THE INDIVIDUATION PROCESS

The individuation process is not easy.

One best apply effort.

> Awareness
>
> Fortitude
>
> Sensitivity
>
> Forthrightness
>
> Honesty
>
> Integrity
>
> Diplomacy

In quiet stillness

In nature

In just Being

Feel the energy of all the trees

Breathe in the air deeply

Take in the filtered sunlight

Meditate on the sun

Watch the spinning sun change colors

A replica of the chakras

Or is it we who mirror the sun?

Forgetfulness

Gold Yellow White Ruby Violet Green Blue

A continuous stream flow of energy

It's sunset now

Time to go home to the soul.

THE SEAL OF MOTHERING THE SOUL

Ave Maria
Holy is the sorrow of the soul of me
Ave Maria
Holy is the sorrow of me
The Eros of Jesus
The Parents of Jesus
The Lighting.

Your healing is over!

The seal of me
The seal of wholeness

The seal of mercy
The seal of even
The seal of losing
The seal of liberty
The seal of mothering
The seal of living
The seal of holiness
The seal of mothering the soul.

WHAT IS POOR

I know the wealth and riches of my God

I know the sorrow of Jerusalem

I know the feebleness of my heart

But Heart of the Sacred

I know not.

Eros knows the secret of me

Eros and Jesus fill the hole in the heart

Eros is the source of love

Eros has not loved the hole in the heart

Await Eros expectantly.

BOUNTEOUS TREE OF LIFE

Bounteous Tree of Life

I come to you for replenishment.

Restore the landmarks of antiquity:

Awe and Wonder.

    You hold a seal

    You hold a wound

    You hold a seal of me

    Open the sea of Eros

    Open the seed of Dabar

    Open the lips of me

    Open the Dabar of me

    Open the sea of me

    Open the sacred of me

    Hold a song of ME.

I shall be transformed in Thy presence Oh God!

LIP SERVICE

Walking on air, being transported, lip service:

I know that you know that we know we are all one in God.

Transformed I must be! All is well. The mighty oak is crooked.

FAITH, DO NOT PERISH BY THE WAYSIDE. I drink the cup of my ancestry,

Bittersweet, until the bud burst full in flower.

GOD EXPRESSED THROUGH US WITH US AND IN US

   Stillness

   Beyond the dawn

   Outbreak

   Ferment

   Holocaust

   Upheaval

   Rent with pain

   Numbness

   Incomplete absurdity

   Focus order and rule

   Diversity

   Subdivision

   Echoes of the past

   Sublimation

   Conjugation

   Internal bliss

I know not whence I came or where I am going.

Utter divine delight, live in the moment. Empty always.

Empty to receive the divine impression/imprint.

Humility to be who I AM. Thank You God.

THE SACRED HEART

The Sacred Heart is ME full-well atoned in bliss and comfort of the Spirit.

Seems strange I didn't know so simple imagery.

How sacred is my life and all wrongdoing too.

I've come to terms: accept the sacred in all, through all and with all.

Love's comfort gives me rest at last, and peace for all eternity.

In paradise I live and breathe, and touch and taste and smell with ears and eyes anew.

ARISE OH SLEEPER

In the stillness a bird chirps, a hammer beats,

The greening of America forever blessed.

The still heart pounds silently, rhythmic balanced.

A cool chill: arise Oh sleeper arise. Wake up the dormant past.

Antiquity bequeaths the wisdom of the heart and soul yearns.

Compassion and greed ever present,

Beyond the sterile wake lies at rest: One with my Maker.

INSANITY NO MORE

Behold the Son of God; behold the son of man.

I am One with my Maker. Alleluia. Joy! Joy! Joy!

Love. Let go and be. Amen. Love ever present,

Embellish my spirit. I seek to be present with my Maker.

Divine light empower ME.

Thou dost bestow Thy grace abundantly.

Effervescence numbed by the clutches of insanity.

Reward the hungry pilgrim journeying.

Divine light, divine grace bestow on me your blessing.

Forth with Thy own power beseech ME/Thee.

Insanity no more: the Easter dawn of Resurrection is here.

Beloved Being Evermore. Mystery enthralls the Wayfarer.

Kathleen David

PART THREE

The pathological norm explodes the myth of power and grace.

THE SECRETS OF THE SOUL
ILLUMINED

PRAYER

That my thoughts will be pure, creative and reflective, always prompted by vision and hope. That my words will speak of your truth and goodness. That my actions will bear the fruits of your example (LOVE).

I do not apologize for awkwardness and clumsiness, for that is part of my very being. My wish is not to insult you. But I do apologize for my stubbornness, resistance and ingratitude to your loving will for me. I must constantly remind myself to "boast of my weakness" and find my strength in you. Jesus taught us by example, that is, loving others as he loved himself. It is through this love that one gains respect and self-discipline.

PERSONAL PHILOSOPHY

Lifestyle changes do lead to health, and make the difference between fully living as opposed to passive existence. A person chooses. One who desires lifestyle change needs to be aware and interested in his own basic human needs. He or she must be motivated to follow through. It may require an alteration of the way he or she perceives reality. A realistic imagination is required to envision the end result. Behavioral and attitude changes are directly linked to self-image and becoming a whole integrated person.

COMMITMENT

Commitment is sharing a bond of love between two people based on faith, hope and trust in God.

LOVE

Humanly speaking, Love is the ability to accept God's love for us.

Love is sharing a bond of intimacy with another person or element in nature. Our chief concern here is people bonds. This bond is not possible without self-love. One cannot love another without some degree of love for self.

The greater the degree of knowledge about another or oneself, the greater the capacity for love. A genuine love relationship fosters a bond of trust. It is free of fear: the greater the love, the lesser the fear.

Generally, men and women have a different approach to love. For men, love is more a matter of the mind followed by the heart. For women, love is more a matter of the heart, then is enlarged and blooms in the mind. There is not a conflict. One complements the other. Both approaches are seen in loving God by the saints.

Love is not possible without acceptance: acceptance of self and others as sinners and saints, acceptance of self and others in weaknesses and strengths. Love requires loving all; loving the weakness but not supporting the weakness. In action, this can appear most harsh. It appears unloving. It is tough. It is knowing how to say NO as well as YES. Sometimes, real love expressed can hurt.

Real love requires forgiveness: forgiveness of self, forgiveness of neighbor and acceptance of God's forgiveness. This cannot be accomplished by man in and of himself. It requires prayer from the heart and makes us realize the helplessness of man and the need for God.

BE DIRECT SINCERE AND HONEST

Do not seek hurt or pain in life. Do not seek defeat. Make choices rather than allow things to happen to you, and therefore feel victimized. Be specific and decisive. Be direct, sincere and honest in relating to self and others. These are elementary steps to loving; loving God, self and others. Anything less is conducive to seeking pain and hurt.

Seek to be in touch with feelings. This can help get one on the right track in life, and is conducive to experiencing fruits of joy, peace and happiness. Remember, joy, peace and happiness are fruits of having been direct, sincere and honest in loving. So called assertiveness is rightfully direct, sincere and honest communication with God, self and others.

Many times, we deny the reality of what is and see as we want things to be. It is important to face denial and deal with it. This is an important aspect of growing and learning to be direct, sincere and honest in relating to God, self and others. One must learn to be his/her own person: that is, who and what he/she is.

THE HEART

Grant me favor, blessing, knowing, clearly perceiving the path I need.

Make clear the way of the Lord. Amen. Thanks be to God.

Open the heart. Love the weakness; embrace it. But do not support the weakness. When weakness is supported, one creates a false relationship. There is a need to develop and nurture fortitude.

REFLECTIONS ON 'LOVE THE WEAKNESS BUT DO NOT SUPPORT IT'

When weakness is supported, one creates a false relationship with oneself, with another person and with God. Therefore, what is good for one is good for all. What is not good for one is not good for all. This is harmonious with Universal and Natural Law.

Openness is needed to avoid fostering false relationships.

    God to Man ... true relationship

    Man to God ... may have false relationship

    Man to Man ... may have false relationship

Communicate and express love. Say what you mean. Do not be a Pillar of the Wound. Fantasy is used to support the wound because genuine communication is not achieved.

The analytical mind takes a look at a past experience. In order to see the reality of the experience, the event needs to be experienced in a milder form. The milder experience is real again. Fantasy and reality are intertwined. They must be separated: the fantasy dropped and reality and vision strengthened.

FEAR AND GUILT

Fear and guilt are a result of lack of self-acceptance and self-forgiveness. If we love our weaknesses, we can see our strengths. They will not be hidden to our mind and eyes.

THE SACRED HEART

You feel evil because of the Sacred Heart. The evil is merciful. The hole in the heart is ME. Eros has not loved the hole in the heart. An open the heart is milk of the Sacred. I AM the Sacred Heart: feminine embodied by Jesus. I AM the hole in the heart. I AM the hole of evil. You owe a death of my heart. You Know that my Soul is a mirror of My Sacred Heart.

THE WAY TO TRUTH

Jesus has shown us the way to seek truth. The Kingdom is within. We must go to the Father, and in Silence hear his message. Each one of us receives a unique message that pertains to our unfoldment. We need to continually seek the silence in prayer and meditation to hear the Word. This gives direction to our lives, purpose and mission. The process unfolds as we learn to be: that is, Be One with the Father.

POOR IN SPIRIT

You are teachable. You are the light of evil. You are the secret of the SOUL. You are the Soul in the heart in love. You are the seed of ME. You know the secret of the simple life. You are in charge of Eros. You are the hope of the illumination of Eros – Love. You are the light of the world. You live a holy life. You live a humble way. Your soul is healed. Your soul is the Savior of Liberty. Lord, have mercy on the Poor in Spirit, now! I am Poor in Spirit.

HEALING FROM THE HOLY SPIRIT

Come Holy Spirit, let my spirit soar and transmute this anger and frustration. Renew my peace. I need to get centered again like the trees and Be. The healing from the Holy Spirit is merely transcending the opposites and becoming a Son of God. I'm working at grounding myself in this way. The emotions interfere sometimes. I'll go home and restore and refresh me. The me still needs much work to be free from negative emotions (wrong attitude). Thank You God for helping me let go of the devils in me.

THE SPIRIT OF TRUTH BECKONED

The Spirit is waiting. The Spirit is mothering the evil/ego. I am home in the Soul. I seek to live more fully in the Spirit. Let this moment be free. Let this moment be empty to hear the Spirit of Truth. The Sun/Son shines brightly.

> Divine Light embrace me
>
> Divine Light enfold me
>
> Divine Light show me
>
> Divine Light lead me
>
> Divine Light protect me
>
> Divine Light embellish my spirit
>
> To Be Who I AM. Amen.

I yield myself to Spirit's desire within ME.

THE ORDER OF DIVINE LIGHT

Brotherhood and Sisterhood are the outward manifestations of stillness mirrored by, through and in our bodies united in spirit, heart and soul. (Eros of the Soul) Jesus is leader, example of the brother and sister in each of us. The androgyny of male/female in each of us expresses through the mirrored male or female body.

DIVINE LOVE

Divine Love flowing in me and through me blesses and multiplies all that I AM, all that I give, and all that I receive, unlimited.

Divine Love flowing in me and through me blesses and multiplies all that I AM, all that I have and all that I AM becoming. Amen. Thank You God. (Note: Unity Prayer variations. Unity Village, MO).

THE EGO

The spirit acts upon the ego to make it strong. The ego is dutiful. The ego is wonderful. The ego is Jesus's way. The ego is waiting, bathing. The mature ego is beautiful (relationship). The ego is the instrument through which the harp is played. This is the love for the SOUL.

I am in harmony with my Divine Self.

THE SOUL OF MYSTERY

The Soul pursues to know and understand its own activity. The Soul clings to error. Profound instincts need to be restored. The Soul is the sorrow of evil. The Soul is the mirror of ME/me. The night of the SOUL is mothering the Satan, the sorrow. The Soul is the home of ME. The soul is the Sacred of ME. The secret of all ages is mothering the evil. The secret is mothering the Soul. The Soul is the altar of God. The Soul is the sacred of all mankind. The Soul is the home of the knowledge of life, liberty and love. The sorrow is the Soul leads the spirit and heart. The Soul is beautiful. The Soul is dutiful. Our Soul needs mothering from evil now. How noble is our Soul. The secret of wholeness is the triumph of the home (Soul). The Soul is the troubadour of the spirit. The Soul is a totally authentic encounter.

My Soul pondereth Thy ways for me

The Soul is healing

The Soul is waiting-bathing

The Soul smiles

My Soul magnifies the Lord

I AM the Divine Light empowered

Grace Honor Glory

Jesus is the Soul

The Soul is the feminine spirituality of God

Working through the Holy Spirit

My Soul is healing through Eros.

EROS

Eros is a holy place of mystery. Eros is the source of love. Eros of OLD is holy. Eros of old is Satan (unwhole). You are in charge of Eros. Eros needs the love of the evil in order to let go of the evil and heal. Eros is the hope of the Soul. Eros is the Soul from ME. The secret of Eros is loving the home of my body. The love which makes desire whole is Eros transformed. Eros knows the hope of deliverance from evil. Eros needs the love of mission for liberty of wholeness. Eros is the Soul of living a joy-filled life. Eros is a song of Dabar in loving a sacred symbol of Dabar. Eros knows the seal of love transformed in the sea of light. Eros knows the sea of light and love of liberty. Eros knows the home/soul of me. The love of Eros knows Dabar in the heart of simply love.

DABAR (CREATIVE PRINCIPLE)

Dabar is a symbol of the soul of Eros in Thee. Dabar is the sacred in the soul. Dabar is the light of day. Dabar is the light of Motherhood. Dabar is the home of martyrdom (surrender) of Thy will be done. Dabar is the sacred in evil/error. Dabar is the seed of ME.

GOD IS

God is stillness, rest, beyond the light, source unlimited, Father, creative principle, the light and life of all, truth perfection, sustaining, infinite Glory, everlasting, eternally, forever Amen. The breath of God is.

> God is love of the heart
>
> God is love of the home
>
> God is love of the Eve of me
>
> God is love of me
>
> Whole, holy is His name, His love, His might, His power.

> Bloom through the heart of ME
>
> You are the hope of ME
>
> Holy Mother of God is the sound of ME.

MORE ILLUMINATIONS

Altar .... is the soul, the pedestal table in church, path, road, a special place for meditation, worship.

Divine Wisdom… is the infinite law of justice: orderly outcome for all creation. It is constant and all-inclusive.

Faith .... is believing and receiving one and the same with honest pure intention of the heart.

Freedom .... is being and doing what you must.

Heel/Heal .... is evil ended in the soul.

Holy Spirit............ is a person in that it is the tiny small voice within that gives us inner guidance to be who we are.

Holy Trinity.......... is the conscience of the Great Trilogy: source of the revelation of Truth.

Hope..................is the soul's beacon light. Hope is a leader. Life in the soul needs hope in ME.

Horror.................is the state of the soul in me.

Individuation........is the process of the birth of the true self.

Joy.....................is a peace beyond me. Joy is peace beyond the mirror of light.

Lord...................is the Son of all humans, the Soul of Jesus, the Soul in You and the Soul of Brotherhood and Sisterhood.

me.....................is young blood's sensuality. YOU are a sequel to me.

Mission...............is the cross of me. The soul is emptied for our mission in life. The light of Love is my mission.

Motherhood.........is the feminine principle of God. The Motherhood of all Humanity is the illumined of the soul. Mothering the Soul is the secret for Humanity.

Mystery...............is the symbol (word) actuated.

New Life.............is home in the heart. A living heart of ME is even, transcending duality of good and evil.

Peace..................is the seed of birthing ME.

Pride...................is the neighbor unfolded in my home (soul).

Savior.................is the milk of the soul. Eros is in a Savior's role. Eros makes me love birthing.

Son of God..........is the Soul of all Humanity.

Tranquility..........is peace/harmony. It is the energy evoked by trees and nature.

Transmutation.....is the process of forgiving love (conversion).

Truth..................is free. What is bound is not part of truth. Truth corrects all error.

Wisdom..............is the knowledge how to live my/our life.

SYMBOL OF HUMILITY THE COLOR OF RUST

I now understand why the color rust is the color symbolizing humility. If we look at nature in the fall and winter, only oak leaves remain on the tree. The oak tree symbolizes faithfulness. But to add the russet leaves (humility) symbolizes the emptying of self; letting go of egocentric qualities to be an open vessel or cup for receiving Faith-knowing.

RAIN EMOTIONS

It rained all day yesterday. The morning is brisk and bright. The rain is like the tears shed to clear the stormy emotions of our psyche. Let us realize the beauty of is-ness. But we have to let go and let go and let go some more. Patience, perseverance, persistence in a nut shell. Fortitude is required.

THE AURA OF THE SUN/SON

I like to meditate on the aura of the sun. The chakra colors are a sight to behold. See the brilliant colors: white, yellow, gold, ruby, pink, violet, blue, green.

> Blue is Power, Protection, Illumined Faith
> Green is Knowledge-Truth
> Ruby-Pink is Divine Love-Healing
> Yellow-Gold is Illumination-Creativity
> Violet is Transmutation-Forgiveness
> White is Purity-Restoration

RING GOLD SUNSET

A ring O fire in Ring Gold
Shines high o'er hill and vale
A ring of fire shoots out its flame
On male and female.

WHAT IS COMMUNION

Real Communion is going within in the silence, and being One with the Father. The Holy Eucharist (bread and wine) is a precious symbol and reality. But the Eros and Dabar ever move us to expand to replace old wineskins with new wineskins, filling them with new wine.

THE WORD

In the beginning was the WORD
And the WORD was with GOD
And the WORD was GOD.

I seek to know and fulfill my mission, whatever that is, in this time and space universe. Amen.

ALL BEING

Snow fallen
Manna from heaven
Birds of the air
Sow and reap the harvest
Pains forgotten
Sorrow sublimated
In the stillness
I see with awe and wonder
To manifest my God
In Thy/my Presence
All being. Amen.

THE JOY OF ME

I will go in unto the altar of God
To God, the Joy of ME!
ALLELUIA, ALLELUIA, ALLELUIA!

LOVE'S WAY

Divine Light
Inspire me to be who I am
Full of love and hate
Greed and solace
Wealth and Riches
The duality of my being
Transformed to become
Who I AM
Love abounds
The Victory has been won
Untold graces
Urge us onward
Shadows lurk in the path
Needless to say
All is well
I AM
I am YOU divine light
And Love unlimited
Wonder, Awe, Embellishment
The drip of the faucet
Becomes a rushing stream
Love's choices, endless
The wounding of the SOUL
Embellishes the Spirit of Grace
The onlooker's choice
To Be, Become
All that I AM, unlimited
Source of light and comfort
Love's way

ECSTASY

Stillness

The Rhythmic Heart Beat

Wonder Awe Grace Granted Bestowed

Light to See Believe Hear Taste Smell Touch

Noise Noiseless

A Bird Echo Call

In the Deep

Profuse

Unadulterated

Sublime

Pure

Ecstasy

UNREDEEMED REDEEMED BLESSED

Gratitude

Gratitude of the heart from the heart

What do you wish to teach me today?

Oblivious Oblivion

Man-made

Stillness Beauty Art

An act of God within

Truth

Forevermore

Unredeemed, ever Blessed

I have compassion for my God

Redeemed, Blessed

Evermore

FEAR

How much I feared Thee
Oh my Lord and God
Tis sad to know that I had
Almost perished in the wake
But now rejoice in joy to
Know Thy grace and love
Eternal.

BIRTHING THE SELF

I need to birth the SELF. What can I do to facilitate birthing? Eros (Spirit-Passion) and Dabar (Soul-Creator) join harmoniously to birth-be authentically Myself-ME.

Eros, come home and grant the Passion and Commitment I need to individuate and express the marvelous God-creation. Thanks.

DREAM

Three identical pictures on different walls.

Divine Self, Empowered, I beseech Thee to bless me with the Grace to be Who I AM. Behold the Brotherhood of Life.

BIRTHING

I will go unto the altar of God.
To God, the birthing of ME.
Our hope is in the name of the Lord.
Who made heaven and earth.
Divine Self, Clarify my innermost desires to make commitment feasible.

The hope of ME is the birthing of anger.
The hope of ME is the birthing of joy.
The hope of ME is the birthing of liberty.

THE SELF

An empty vessel
I/You create
Love's desire embellished by fruit
Oh yes, nay. A watchman's stand
Ah! Fellowship encountered
Post-gleaming bright
Desires bliss foretold
I do not Know
Creation gods on
In streams of decadence
Foretold. Pray tell.
Honor's delight, ambiguous
All knowing creed of acceptance
Sway to and fro
Silence Awe and Wonder
Graced by the Glorious Resurrection
Decaying wood. Gnarled branch
Ripening fruit gush forth
A symbol of integrity, honesty, forthrightness

Change of action patterns
A new birth! The SELF
Unencumbered by all that is.

BEING

All too soon cross links cross
Creative power and glory
One being in Thee. All is well.
Sustenance, beholden to a deity
Mesmerized, drunken
Abide in me, Oh Lord
A race of consequence
I see to be Thee empowered
Richness Fellowship Old Wine
Renewed in Hope
Truth, bountiful, glistening, radiant
All ways, all present forevermore
Let go and BE
Be ME, Amen
Thank you, God
The Dress, Robed in splendor. RADIANT BEING.

THE DAWN BREAKS

Almighty God, have mercy on your children. How can we be so clueless and out of touch with Thee. Your beauty abounds.

>Dear God, I long to be one with Thee
>I AM one with Thee
>Unrecognized
>A language unspoken, unheard
>I seek Thee with wonder and awe
>I create anew with Thee
>In stillness, in silence
>IN, through and with
>The Divine Presence. Amen.
>Thank you, God.

>The dawn breaks.

GIFTS OF THINE OWN MAKING

Divine Love, flowing in me and through ME blesses and multiplies all that I AM, all that I have and all that I receive, unlimited.

I ask my divine Self to orchestrate my delivery in time of need. Thank you, God.

>Being, that as IAM
>Filled, Full, Fruitless
>Behold Son of God

>Transform the moment into rich Supply

>Drink with Thine Eyes

Eat with Thine Ears
Grant me rest in the Spirit
Rest assured
Gifts of Thine own making bud forth
For all mankind

Thank you, God.

SUPPLICATION

Behold, Lamb of God
I beseech Thee
Thou wilt aid in my endeavors.

Balancing is difficult for me. Art, Beauty, Truth, Love, Justice, Compassion; These are essential ingredients in my life. I need greater simplicity to achieve this end. I seek to develop RITUAL conducive to my being. Help me to be rid of the unimportant.

>Divine Love, Embrace me
>>Inspire me
>>Enfold me
>>Protect me
>>Strengthen me
>>Empower me
>
>To be who I AM.

FREEDOM

I seek birthing New Life
Freedom to be
And do as I must.

ABOUND IN ME OH GOD FOREVER

Tis Thee my Son. But pray,
Behold the Son of God, Son of Man
I am with Thee always, all ways. Amen.
After being driven out of the town of Egypt
I am one with my Spirit, my God, my All
Unto Thee/me is the Resurrection
Glorious unto all forever, Amen.

Abound in me Oh God forever. For I am AM
Thee crucified again and again.
Albeit in the midst of turbulence and fraud.
I succumb to Thy/My wishes: Deep wishes of the heart.

Abundant flow of grace
The wishes of the heart fulfilled
Forever abiding in Thee/me. Amen.
Truth abounds.

CENTERING

The trees calm me. The birds and nature calm my vexed spirit. I need this tranquility to create divinely. Thank you God for your beautiful creation.

REBELLION

We need to rebel and be angry too when our balance is overridden and threatened and correct it. That's what I seek to do.

This day, I seek to know again Who I AM, to be in touch. I desire to create divinely to bring harmony and peace within and to this world.

SCREAMS FOR VICTORY

Oh broad streams of pleasure
The smells of Mother Earth
The fragrance of the flower and leaf
The sounds of birds
The insects swarming
The dew drops billowing glow on green
Dreams of wonder orient my Soul
To beauty, cause and effect
Blistering hot, the scorching of my feet
To let my attention grasp the moment of relief
In cool refreshing waters of antiquity.

The screwdriver, the scissors the knife that
Cuts the umbilical cord of destruction.
Must I admit defeat in vain pleasures?

At last, some sense is made of autonomy
Crude wisdom replaces death sentence
Oh Mother, reach out and touch Thy Child, Puer
The Christ within screameth for Victory
Not gentle, not sweet…But harsh and cruel

To reach cold hearts to stir anew
Reach out and blast the present state.

Oh Wisdom, merciful and bountiful
Your just reign seeketh to restore, renew

        Mother Earth
        Mother Wisdom
        Mother God
        Mother Justice
        Mother Truth

In a new world order.
Thanks be to God! Amen.

THE SECRET OF YOU IS ME

This night I rest in peace and love unduly
You live the life of ME.
The secret of you is ME.

AWAKE OH SLEEPER AWAKE

Awake Oh sleeper awake
Arise Oh sleeper arise
Relinquish the dormant past
In bold emanations walk
The time is short
Heed my warning call
My Presence will not be thwarted

Forgive and Be

Be Who Thou Art

The power and glory of God's Kingdom

Bud forth

Ready or not

So be it. Amen. Alleluia!

I AM

Tell me there is no way but to fall in the midst of the prey of wolves
YOU ARE WHOLLY FEEBLE. I AM I AM!

THE LORD SHALL TEAR OPEN THE SACRED VEIL

The Lord shall erase animal

And man shall no more know/love evil

The Lord shall love Me me

The breath of God is

Open the temple of the holy Song of ME

Open the even me. Open the light of me.

The SOUL is the mirror of the home

The SOUL needs a Faithful way.

THE RAPE OF THE CENTURY

You were a Soul of Lies

Hold a vision of Love

You are a SOUL of ME

You are a soul of Being

You are a soul of even

The Soul is the home/hope of ME
The Love of ME is the home in ME
The SOUL loves, the SOUL hopes
I live a holy Eros.

BIRTHING THE DIVINE ENERGY IN THE WORLD

BEAUTY	RITUAL
ART	TRUTH
MUSIC	ORDER
CULTURE	RULE

HONOR – human focus – DISCIPLINE

UNDERSTANDING THE PROCESS

The evil heart impregnates the soul. The soul never knew the sin of the heart. You are a secret of loving me now. I AM the soul in ME. The Sacred. The soul makes a leap of consciousness that eliminates the fear.

Lord, I am not worthy is a trial in the sorrow (Jerusalem) in me now. Then we have Eros fill the hole in the heart. Then we have Jesus fill the hole in the heart. You are a seat of the SOUL in me. My SOUL is the safer place for the sacred in me. My love for evil is the love of EVEN. Eros is lonely. The hole in the heart wants. You are the seal in the sea of love. The Seal of Love.

The Soul is the Soul of ME now. You are the soul of me now. You are the soul of Eros.

Holy Mystery of God, pray for me to be the SOUL of Thee. Amen.

Our soul is from God. (angered SOUL)

'God' loathed the angels for rebelling in PRIDE. Cast out, this evil ravaged MAN.

Mary and Joseph carried the Christ Child by their YES to preserve the simple life of Joy in me – ME – GOD.'

Our prayer is for the forgiveness of all evil, that all life be spared and the wounds be consumed in the fire-flame (of LOVE),

Our pain is part of this fire.

We are no longer in the law of KARMA. We are in the law of LOVE.

I WAS THE SLAVE IN THE SECRETS OF THE SOUL

The soul is in need of my heart. The soul is the/my sorrow transformed in love and in me. The deliverance of EVEN is the heart of me, a living Heart of ME. The heel of the Soul is evil ended.

SECRETS OF THE SOUL ILLUMINED

We each are mythmakers if we authentically express the SELF of who we are. I AM the Divine source of Light. You are the bridge in ME. The secret of the Soul is horror to the Soul in light. The Eros is in a Savior's role. The Eros makes me love birthing. Our One Being with God is Immanent. New Life is the home in my heart.

The Earth is a House of Prayer. We have turned it into a den of thieves. Our body temple is the House of God. Rejection of the body puts a limit on the Spirit.

Wisdom is the knowledge how to live our lives.

The manifestation of the Spirit comes through diligent effort and calm. I live alone in ME. Spirit is the light of ME of the SOUL.

There is prejudice in Being. Religion has come to an idol consciousness.

You are the feel of ME – emotions – compassion – love. I AM the even. YOU are the secret of the SOUL. I have come to honor the simple way of ME.

I/YOU WILL the SOUL of ME. I/YOU WILL the SON of ME.

To lift the world, I have to birth the wholesome ME. The seed of evil loves a soul. The sloth of me abhors the truth, hallowed be the rules, the divine rule of mercy and love. The paradoxical claim of churches is heretofore strengthened. But the divine light and wisdom shower on us the everlasting Truth, the gospels of Truth. You hold my Seal of my horror of me.

BEHOLD THE SON OF GOD

Our Father who are the living ME, hallowed by my home. I AM the divine light empowered. Behold the Son of God.

The soul is the light of ME. Death of the soul of Eve is a lonely way. To mirror the light requires death of the soul.

OUR FATHER TRANSPIRED

Our Father who are me
Thou art the Son of me
Our faith is in the SOUL.

Our Father who art me
Hallowed Souls of Thee/me.
Live a soul of me.

Our Father live us.

Our Father love us. The whole me loves.
Our Father help us lead the Soul of Thee.

Our Father who art in me.
You are the seal of me.

You are the Soul in the Heart
You are the Hole in the Heart
I AM the SOUL in the HEART of ME
The Resurrection of my Spirit ever Glorious unto Thee. Amen.

You are the living ME
I AM the seal of ME.

You are a deliverer of mirroring the light and love of ME;
the light and love of Eros.
You are the deliverer of ME now. You are the I. You are a Lion.
The Lion is the Holy One.

A NEW WORLD ORDER

The marble mansions of Zion
The quicksilver of trust
The brethren flocked
Misnamed
Mansions of Zion
We explore the possibility of a new regime

The mark of ME
It is your life of high altar
This is the opening of the Seal.

New Life is the home in my heart
Lamb of God, You who take away the sin of the world
Restore our innocence.
The Soul is the Mater-Pater of ME, the Son
The Soul is the Our Father in ME.
He has defined You in a new way
You are the Soul of ALL LOVE
You are a new world order
My peace is the seed of birthing ME.

PART FOUR
Once the Soul is even, the Karmic pattern is ended.

Circle of Completion

MATTERS OF THE HEART:
A NEW BEGINNING

MATTERS OF THE HEART: A NEW BEGINNING

> I will go in unto the altar of God
>
> To God the Joy of ME
>
> Our help is in the name of the Lord
>
> Who made heaven and earth
>
> I seek to be Who I AM The God within.

PROLOGUE TO MATTERS OF THE HEART
EROS

Eros is the early part of ME

Eros is the end of the soul

Eros is the birth of Me: the soul of Me, the Soul of Eros

Eros is end of home in the soul.

Feeling

Fear of ME is

Eros and Dabar are hearing the spirit.

Eros is

Eros is humble of Me

Eros is brother of Me

Eros knows the sword of Me

Eros knows liberty

Eros is lamb when he is bridled: that is, he has come home and stays home in the SOUL

Eros needs the liberty and love of 'me' for all mankind

Eros is the secret of holiness

Grant us the wholeness of Eros in Jesus.

Eros is in a Savior's role

Eros makes me love birthing

Eros is the Soul of Me now

Eros is the Soul of Jesus

Eros is the hope of Me now

No one is evil

Eros knows the soul life is home of the heart.

BRIGHT SUNSHINE OH HAPPY DAY!

Once the soul is EVEN, it has died a certain death. A resurrection ensues: resurrection of Eros. This Eros is divine and provides the passion-ecstasy to be the true self: that is, to share the gifts in the concrete world that activate our purpose and mission in life. This becomes real, realized. We dig up from the well what is ours to give, to share in making the world a better place to live.

The heart of the matter:

Eros Come home Stay home

Accept your bridle and rein! The soul cries

Steadfast ground; Be it so

Alter not the path

Provoke not the thought

Empty Always empty to receive

Thy divine impression, imprint

And be who you are

Unlimited in faith, prestige, courage

Unprecedented wealth and riches

Of Being.

This acceptance of the bridle and rein by Eros (coming home to the soul) is the stage of "containment." *C.J. Jung*

My greatest need is to experience the individuation: the birth of the true self. Thank You God for granting me this deep wish of the heart.

EVIL AND SIN

Evil is that existent force compelling man to be what he is not. This force is demonic. Being human takes part through, with and in the divine: God is! Evil is personified by an entity: Satan Devil. Why is so much of man today pursuing to be what he is not?

Man loathes the body. This is translated into self-hate and destruction: destruction to self, to others and to Mother Earth. What is needed, what is called for is mothering the evil woundedness to heal the soul of me and others. This mothering the evil is the secret of all ages.

THE HOLY SPIRIT

The Holy Spirit is a person in that it is the tiny small voice within that gives us inner guidance to be who we are. The Holy Spirit, this communion between Father and Son in rest-stillness is that point of oneness-interdependence expressed in the most profound and holy sense. This requires listening, being, not doing.

> "Out of the depths I cry to you Oh lord
>
> Have mercy on me, a sinner."

The soul on its own is steeped in error and confusion. Without the marriage of the Soul with Eros, one cannot express the fullness of the divine. This union is the nature of man to become fully alive and fully human. It is this individuation process that is needed and will transform the world. This process confirms: The secret of Eros is evil transformed.

    Lord, hear our prayer and supplication. Amen.

Out of the depths Oh sinner arise

Behold thy Being, sacred and whole

Conform to the image and likeness of whom Thou art

Blessed be thy name

Fulfill the prophecy of old

Grace granted. Peace be with Thee/Me

Manifest thy Being

Enjoy the wake

Behold the Sons of God.

Thank You God for Your gifting ME

I love You/Thee.

I DON'T KNOW THEE AS I OUGHT

Out of tumult, out of weariness, I behold Thee, my Son
I am one with Thee: Ever beseech Thee, ever ridicule Thee
I don't know Thee as I ought
I come before the throne, angelic hosts, ever blessed be Thy grace
Permit me indulgent awakening
The constancy of prayer and supplication unbidden by defeat.

MOTHERING THE EVIL

Mothering the evil is the secret of all ages. What does this mean? It means loving our weaknesses, but not supporting these weaknesses. There is a divine order in our universe expressed in natural law and divine law. These laws are harmonious without our being. When these laws are violated, we have chaos and upheaval: destructive forces operative that deprive man from realizing who he is and what his purpose is. There is extreme suffering.

The evolutionary unfolding of man to cosmic consciousness is blocked and delayed when he refuses to obey these laws: that is, act in harmony with his nature and purpose. The prophetic voice is called for to admonish the sinner. (less than human – steeped in error).

We live in relationship: relationship with God, with self, with one another, with Mother Earth and the entire universe. This relationship is governed by natural and divine law. Its characteristics are: Oneness, Interdependence. Through harmonious being, we find our way home: our way home to the SOUL!

I AM ONE WITH THEE MY GOD

I am one with Thee my God
Blessed be Thy/My name to whomever it is sent
Bestow the wicked erroring Thy grace and light anew
Dispel the fears of turbulent man.
    Arise Oh child arise
    Your cosmic glory beckons you to behold a deity unfettered
    Whimsical encounters. Unerring in Thy grace
    Behold the Sons of God! Return to paradise, the promise of antiquity.
I behold the magnitude of my God

I behold a deity

I walk with grace and awe and splendor

Embellished by the light and love of God's embrace. Thank You God.

THE DIVINE PLAN

No longer shrouded in mystery, my fears of Thee dispelled

For most a life time I feared Thee

A fear so rent with grief and pain my soul cried out for truth

Revealed to be at last through thorns and wounds

Of my encumbered past.

Break forth the steeplechase anew at one with The eternally

In heart, soul, mind and strength of the Christ within

For all humanity, I pray Thy light and love and power anew

It's up to us to choose the Divine Plan of love and light

To serve the Will of God to serve the will of ME. Thank You God.

PURPOSE AND MISSION

The beauty of the season beckons me. I am in wonder, awe and question. To whom does God appropriate the means I relish? Fatigue sets in. No play.

The sunset of my relationship, the dawn of newness. I seek to relinquish old ways. I seek to eliminate those tasks, jobs, duties, obligations, responsibilities that are not conducive with following through with my purpose. My purpose is to carry out my mission. My mission is my cross. My mission is to be poor in spirit. My mission is to love the soul SOUL. Now, what do I do to orchestrate harmony and peace?

I go in unto the altar of God
To God the Joy of ME.

HOMELESSNESS

"When an inner situation is not made conscious,
it appears outside as fate."
C. G. Jung

Today, more than ever before, we are overwhelmed by homelessness – worldwide. If we apply Jung's theory, how is homelessness, that is, people living in the streets with no house, apartment, trailer, room or abode of some sort to call home, seen as fate?

In our electrical universe, we now understand what we are in a world of opposites. In considering this case, some people have a home and some people do not have a home to live in. The more finely tuned our consciousness is, the greater is the illumination or understanding of the meaning of home and homelessness.

I suggest that because we have become so "lost" we do not understand the deeper meaning of "home." The true meaning of home is GOD as expressed by the poet Wordsworth in the closing lines…"From God, who is our home." Knowing this does not reveal a clear simple solution for our electrical body. However, it can begin to show us the right direction to move. The place to find God is in the soul. In order to find Jesus in the soul, we have to open the heart, and allow ourselves to be touched by the Holy Spirit. We each have to take responsibility to invite Jesus into our lives. With this goes the stripping and the emptying of our personal and collective garbage. Our true home in the human-divine sense is the soul.

Homelessness, worldwide, provides a mirror to show us that most of us are lost and not at home in the soul. When we take this giant step, that is, come home to the soul, we will see a change in our concrete world.

> We will become counter cultural
>
> We will act out brotherly love, that is, share on an equitable level
>
> We will live simply
>
> We will live in wonder and awe
>
> We will love the soul SOUL.

I propose that the absence of genuine mothering has created an imbalance in the world. The patriarchal regime has steered off course into oppression and domination. We are victims of this long-lived regime and the only clear way to recovery is: Prayer Meditation Conversion.

Our dear Blessed Lady (Mary, Mother of Jesus) has been telling us this message for years. She is our stronghold, our hope. She is our mirror to show us the dire need for MOTHERING the EVIL (Satan, error, weakness, sin or however you wish to name it) but NOT SUPPORT IT!

This means:

GRACE	Be open to GRACE	Open the HEART
HONOR	Honor the SACRED in EVIL	Forgive and Repent
GLORY	Allow TRANSFORMATION by the Holy Spirit	Glorify God

We need to seek transformation in the healing presence of love and light.

OUR FATHER

Our Father, I am in awe and wonder
Your blessings and grace abound
In humble awakenings I stand
Behold me ME.
I desire to be who I AM.

How blessed is Thy curse
Of pain and suffering
To bring us new light to see the hold
May I be fitting to be who I AM
One with Thee. Amen.

WHEREVER MY HEART IS GOD YOU ARE A SONG OF DABAR

My healing heart belongs to you
Of grace bestowed limitless
Behold. I AM
I AM ME preponderant always all ways
The moment of grace is gone
You are a deity unbeknown to you
Throw light on the truth revealed
Overcome with joy, the phantom dissipated
Innermost being revealed reveals who Thou art
Go on, Move on
Be who Thou art, manifested in ME
All being and glory for the Kingdom
Show forth. You are one with ME
I AM. I AM ME
Ever present to the Holy Spirit
Bleeding hearts cooled by the flames of LOVE
Whither Thou goest, all is well.

THE HOUSE! WHAT OF THE HOUSE?

The house. What of the house? Do you not know?

This abode is Mine

Filled with grace and awe and wonder.

I come before Thee my Lord. Burdened

"I can do all things through Christ who strengthens Me"

Eros of God, You who take away the sins of the world

Receive our prayer of thanksgiving.

HOW SHALL I /WE RESPOND TO GRACE

Go forth. Be. Be a light of wisdom and truth

Evermore. Beseech not

Your armor is the Word. The Word of God spoken

In lust humbly laden aside, a willing Spirit buds forth

Unkept, unclean, the world knows no Savior

In the recesses of the heart, in the midst of temples and synagogues

I display the wonder of Eros as LAMB

Thanks be to God. Amen.

UNIVERSE REVEAL YOUR SECRETS FOR ME TO ME

Universe, reveal your secrets for me to me. I seek to integrate my animus within me – not to project it onto others. I seek to awaken the dormant power of divine love and grace within me to fully express myself and be who I am.

Be clear and know that I AM God!

I AM a deliverer from evil in the home of Eros

I AM a deliverer of love, liberty and light

Mothering the evil – woundedness heals the soul of me and others

I AM a light to the SOUL

Deliverance from evil is the light of the SOUL

The secret of all ages is mothering the SOUL

Eros needs the liberty and love of ME for all mankind.

My mission is to lead the poor in soul to love the SOUL. I seek to embrace Life. I wish to sit back – pray – wait for the direction of the Holy Spirit.

> Speak Lord, I'm listening
>
> Thank you God for your Beauty
>
> I AM in awe and wonder.

REBIRTH

Dreams of past enterprise stop boldly in my tracks

The moments stillness brings New Life

The blank mind receives a new creation: Stillness Awe Wonder Beauty Truth

I AM one with my Maker. Behold! A glorious resurrection.

Assurances repeated again and again

Can I assimilate the newness of Be Become Becoming all that I AM meant to be

No longer separated from Life of Life through Him with Him and in Him

Manifested in My own Being, Son of God?

Dreams of past yearnings no longer needed
The glory of God shines forth
Alms taken. The Wayfarer beholds uncertainty
Confidence in my Master.   My Being   My One   My All.

Dreams of past Offerings
Subtle Subtlety
Thank You God for Infinite Divine Mercy and Love
Unbroken past.   Sublimated   Rejuvenated   Reborn.

REFLECTIONS ON DESIRE

I seek and love much solitude. It is necessary for me to evolve, develop and fulfill my mission. I experience lots of tension. I am torn between hands on work and developing my true self.

I seek divine guidance of the Holy Spirit to protect me, guide me, lead me in the specific directions, details and areas that are right for me and in total harmony with my divine self.

I thank you God for gifting me and raising my consciousness. I praise You and openly express my desire to listen, learn, express and share with the world in making our world a 'Paradise' orchestrated by your divine love and presence.

I desire to live in the Presence of the Kingdom. Lord, grant me your rest, favor and blessing. I love You Thee. I love ME. Thank You God.

PROCESS

Doubts and transgressions, purgatorial delight

Manifests itself in the recesses of the heart

The soul knows truth

Eros, awakened in the soul leads the Truth, Being, At-one-ment

The heart, driven by imagination gets in trouble and creates error.

Eros, centered in the Soul calls forth justice

This process, becoming, stirs Eros to fire passion in the heart

To fulfill destiny – purpose – mission.

    Oh Divine Delight, I embellish my spirit

    To Be Become One with Thee. Amen.

GUIDANCE BY DIVINE LIGHT

I am guided by Thy divine light

Ever be it manifested in my heart

Overwhelmed with grief and sadness

Dissipated by the storms of glory evermore.

All too soon the rocket blast:

My Kingdom come, Thy will be done

On earth as it is in Thee.

Give us this day our daily bread

And forgive and Be.

Be One with Thee – ME. Amen.

THE SOUL'S WISDOM

Dawn breaks. What is this! I say overload creates resentment. Clarity of Mind and purpose, I seek. Thwarted paths are obstacles to overcome. BE!
Dismayed, unforgiven of obscenities, the Soul's wisdom is man's greatest seeking. Beauty and Truth ever present express the inexpressible in words not so clear. We must go on and Be. Pursue the unknown, in trust.

I'm seeking to simplify, simplify, simplify. I need my Higher Self to direct and steer me. The birds are free and cheerful. I want to be joyful and free and enthusiastic like them.

LESSONS TAUGHT IN BEING

Deep within my loins, the gridiron of past embraces my inmost desire: Being. Being, that as I may and do, I seek fellowship with old wine to teach me new lessons in Being. Oh girded loins of strength and antiquity, I beseech Thee to rescue me from present torment: torment of my soul in yearning to be Who I AM.

I bogged down in clutter and obligations of this time and age and place seek to be freed from the clutter that imprisons me. I seek to be constantly in the awe and presence of my Maker, my divine breath of Life. I AM One with Thee! But I must feel this in my soul, in my cells, in my total Being: my heart, my soul, my mind, my strength.

Oh sweet Mystery of Life, let me in each moment be filled with awe and wonder and grace to be continually transformed in Thee. Amen.

I am seeking to live this New Life abundantly. Yes, little wonder. Of graces bestowed so bounteously. How can I forget Who I AM?

LOVE'S EMBRACE

I bestow my blessing concomitantly. Behold the Lamb of God, Eros of God, You Who take away the sins of the world, Have mercy on me. As we forgive, You forgive. Enormity relinquished, I desire to be Who I AM.

The moment is now. Lend an ear. Be of service. Call on Thy divine Self empowered. Holy is Thy sepulcher. What is wanting is grace. Bestow favor on Your servant – Servants, Lord. Trust in Faith, Faith in the process. BE.

Divine source of wisdom and light, Descend on me, your brethren. I am open, not as a can of worms, but as Thee empowered with grace and power through Your most Holy Spirit. I command. I AM. I BE. One with Thee.

Grant me faith knowing to fulfill Thy wishes. Glory be to the Father, Son and Holy Spirit. I command the presence of my Maker fortified with the strength to lift the deluge of defeat. Lord, I pray that Your Holy Will – DIVINE WILL be My Will in this encounter, blessing: LOVE's embrace.

ALL BEING WITH ONE

The dawn breaks. Again I see new light: Being One with my Maker. Peace bestowed upon me. I run for seclusion. I make amends. I falter not. I am growing to be Who I AM. Concomitant example. Rest assured.

All Being with One, In One, Through One; in the name of Jesus Christ, Our/My Lord and Savior. Amen.

MIRROR THE LIKENESS OF THEE

Dreams of yesteryear, quiet stillness, silence, awe and wonder. A chirping bird of the air proclaims His Majesty's delight. Ever forthcoming, blessed be Thy grace/gift. Recompense for past mistakes to mirror the likeness of Thee, and be Who I AM. Amen.

PRAYER OF THANKS

Thank You God. I continue to seek your guidance and wisdom moment by moment. I love You, Thee, ME. Amen. Grant healing and blessing on your people: sheep without a shepherd. We are/have been blind to your perfect guidance. Thank You for correcting us and establishing the divine order which brings us altogether in One Peace, Love, Wholeness, Divine Worship. Amen.

EXISTENTIAL WORSHIP

Existential worship oft sublimated to the whims of our fancy

The reality blocked amid confusion

Stripes of error, garbage in the heart.

May we succumb to the profound blessings of Truth and Worship. Amen.

WARFARE OF SPIRIT AND SOUL

The soul cries and rebels, enough is enough.

I want to be free and manifest the real ME!

This is not automatic. It takes effort, energy, time, silence.

Behold the Son of God – ME – established through warfare

Warfare of spirit and soul in juxtaposition.

BALANCE

Thank You God for clarity of purpose: forthright, albeit unfettered
Balance. Balance. Balance. This is the key to unlock the doors.
The seed sprouts in throws of restlessness.
Peace obliterates the strain, the torment of opposition to birth who
I AM! Amen.

THE WAY OF THE WARRIOR

I speak the way of the Warrior, known not to man.
Albeit well justified, sincere and heart rendering,
My gift of love ever reaches and resides within myself: Total Being.

THE MYSTERY OF ME

The mystery of ME is ongoing, wherewith my God and my Maker.
Mother and Lover of Even, I pursue the unknown.
The temple of wrath set aside, I Being one with Thee ever blast the falsity
To become who I AM. Thank You God.

I sit like the bird perched on the windowsill: Be. Being all One in Thee.
I live, breathe, ever extending myself, my Being to Oneness in Thee.
This interchange, still new to me seeks to extend to You/Thee.

> All. One. Unified in diversity. Awe and Wonder.
> Grace expressed in the inexpressible.
> Fathom of my Being, Beingness.
> Joyful gladness, merriment, play, the Puer, childlike simplicity.
> Innocence – dawn of freshness.
> Awakened to behold in ME – Thee. Amen.

DISCOVERY

Discovery. Awe of creation. Co-creation. Paradigm delight:

Surging forth like rapids in the stream.

Not chaotic, but channeled, focused orderly, disciplined

From that deep reservoir of the God-consciousness.

The Puer comes forth to play and be my Playmate: each moment NEW.

I am observer and observed.

BELIEF

I AM the divine child too, ever present in the abyss.

I long for communion. Bleating moments I do not comprehend.

Awareness of grace.

I believe in the Trinity: in ME.

BE STILL

Ever present, moments of grace.

Be! Still the waters of unknown depths.

I unencumbered proclaim:

>This is the WAY the Lord has made.

>Let us be thankful and glad.

Merriment of heart. Screeching brakes: the temporal scene.

Be still and know that I AM God.

EROS AS LAMB. EROS OF GOD.

I write in the midst of chaos and plunder. I believe in who I AM. All too soon the rockets blast. Let us grow in love in Thy Presence.

Noises proliferate. Wealth of nation's abhor the power of Being.

It is inevitable, the grace of essence:

> the flower, the bird, the tree, the rock, the child, the woman, the man, Puer and Senex, once again united in wholeness in Being – ONE.

Unending wealth and riches in the depths of my Being. Unexplored by most of us, I surge forth like the lion to renew the hope of the lamb: lost sheep in the wilderness to discover Eros as Lamb.

> Lamb of God Eros of God
>
> You Who take away the sins of the world
>
> Have mercy on us.

Eros of God transformed in rightful measure to bring forth the Kingdom of God within. We are the missing likeness of Jesus the Christ to herald in the new World Order.

> Peace be with you. Peace be with us. Peace be with ME.

PLANETARY BEING

I see the world anew, planetary Being uppermost, grounded in the depths of my nature; the clay formed and molded to become, become who I AM. I, single of purpose and mission, I, the Wayfarer grounded to become the Presence of God.

I look to my neighbor. All is One, unity in diversity of being; my loving God of variety, awesome splendor. I riding on wings of spirit humbly proclaim:

Be whom Thou Art! Reverence for me. Reverence to all that is.

Mirroring, always, all ways, my God my Maker.

Be that as it may, I instinctively call you to the divine embrace. Join in the fellowship and grace of being One with ME/Thee:

Exuberant Joyful Playful Creator and Being as One.

Eros and Dabar fully expressing the inexpressible

Through clay formed and molded in perfection of Being.

Thank You God.

WITNESS OF LIGHT BEARING LOVE

I desire to be who I AM, That witness of light bearing love to, with and in the universe. Appeal I must, to the higher realms. Far/for be it. Untold, modern grace to be who I AM.

Thank You God for showing me the Way and the Light and Life of my SOUL. I in juxtaposition acclaimed by posterity in the realms of fairies and queens. I, Queen of the May, Springtime apple-blossomed beauty, fettered, untorn, untold; the mystery of resurrection: birth of a deity, past slumbering, long forgotten memories, enjoy the birth, the wonder, the awe, the commitment, the grace to be who I AM. Amen. Thank You God.

THE TRUE ME

Discovery, beyond the world of perception, beholden to a King/Queen deity, I creator, co-creator with my God. I distraught with ambivalence: decisions paramount, healing love to me and my Maker, anger of my soul squelched by needed victory. Quietude, albeit dumbfounded bliss, peace manifold. Love. Let go and be. Be One with Thee. Amen.

Deep within the reservoirs of my Being, still waters submerge with the life-giving force of my God: letting go of old patterns, creating the empty vessel, to receive my being One with Thee. Dissipated energies flow gracefully to embody the spirit within. Curtailed dreams unfold. The mysteries expose and reveal the true ME. Thank You God.

INNER TRUTH – MATTER OF THE HEART

Inner truth, a matter of the heart manifold, manifested

In the wake of deliverance from evil (error). Told. Grace granted.

Deliverer of light and love dissipated in the reaches of obscurity;
Illuminated in dispelling fear of foreboding Truth.

Deluge. Can it be that I am so vulnerable to be awakened to the torment
Of the Soul? Pray come now. Albeit past rendered in service and love,

I tempted to be one apart from Thee. A repetitive act needed to be consummated in the wellspring of the heart.

THE KINGDOM WITHIN

I am inspired to be who I AM in the midst of tribulation, foreseen only

With the eyes of God. Thank You God. If I, lacking in faith in the

Beingness of my soul, penetrate the darkness and fear; reach out and permeate

My Being with Truth, I encompass all Being ever present, controlled by

No one but the self-expressed Kingdom within. Perfection granted, manifold,

Ever-present to mirror to express the divine within.

PERFECTION GRANTED TO ALL BEING

I see perfection granted to all Being. How marvelous a concept.

A revelation to the host of my Being, whence I come startled to awaken the soul within to respond to the wellspring of Nature: joy and mirth, gladness of heart. My soul embellished in the wake of forgetfulness. No longer encumbered in my Being. Amen.

MOTHER OF EVEN THE FEMININE PRINCIPLE OF GOD

My desire of the heart is to quicken the Spirit to respond to the perfection of Oneness in Thee: albeit rendered in love, light and simplicity of heart. Duality no more expressed in my Being, I AM Mother of even, the feminine principle of God.

Ah yes, Spirit embellished. How grateful a deity to remember who I AM: Newness, new born Being to encompass the old, the Truth of antiquity. Yes, the mystery of Life revealed to please my Maker. Amen.

THE CHRIST

Immaculate conception, Queen of the May

Birth of Truth splendorous in Thy/My Being

Break of dawn! Light manifested

Understanding who I AM! In humility

Humbly awakening to the Truth of my Being

Activity activated. The Christ.

EVOLUTIONARY AWAKENING

I the Wayfarer Breathe in the light, the air:

The furnace of desire, heart's embellishment made golden,

Glimpses of the mundane emanating boldly to disclose ever reaching obscenity

To diversity of Being, Long-lived past awakened in the slumber of forgetfulness.

Albeit divine and orderly, out of chaos and plunder; ridiculed by man, obscene sublime. We are all bent in the direction of intercourse – divine or otherwise. I slow to bend the reed in the wind evolve to greater awakening of the heart and spirit. Thank You God.

RESPONSE TO MY MENTOR THE CHRIST

The golden realm of idols and kings, I joy filled Being

Accept the gift of fate obliterated by the Sea of Divine embrace.

Divine Embrace, mocked by man, explode the myth of power and grace.

I encounter the angels' awakening to behold my Spirit One with Thee.

Of what further avail is the avalanche of success, awakening to hostile encounter?

I succumb to the blessings of my Being: being One with Thee.

I know not whence the tree has fallen to such a state in remorse and grief.

Can it be to no avail? I need the space and time, the quietude

To reflect on my Being. I no longer victim must choose to Be.

My destiny cries out to be One with my Maker.

The catapult of desire, the precipice of reason,

The foreboding truth dispels the fear of Being.

I no longer innocent, ignorant respond to the call of my Mentor, the Christ.

The clutter, the garbage must go. The distractions, the interruptions must abate.

Time is running out. My call to myself is my call to you, my neighbor. Share and commune with me to be One with our Maker.

> Let go of past hurts, wounds. Be One with Me/Thee now:
>
> This moment of grace, this moment, everlasting. Amen.
>
> My children have suffered through trial and torment.
>
> The union is commensurate with My Spirit.

NONCOMMITTAL COMMUNION WITH ALL IN SOLITUDE

In the deep silence of my Being I participate in the communion of all:

Of One in, through and with All. I enhanced by the flavor of existential worship

Am compelled to proceed noncommittal.

Life's discovery, a unique journey for each

Soul to blossom forth, untainted by the so-called wisdom of foolhardy men.

I in solitude seek my God, my Maker: Truth untainted, unspoiled.

Communal penance demystifies the mystical – makes clear the way of the Wayfarer.

I commune with Nature, my God-Being in solitude.

JOY OF RESURRECTION

My soul troubled by the clutter

The cluttered pain of being less than I AM.

The sun shines forth to dissipate my fears.

Anger stored in labyrinths of the Soul

Dissipated by the newness to come: Being One with Thee.

Committed to Truth ever blessed, foreboding glimpses rendered fruitless,

The Joy of Resurrection takes hold to balance One with Thee/ME.

Amen.

BEING ONE WITH THEE

I go into the labyrinths of my Soul to seek awareness of Thy/MY Being.

The comforts of apostasy forfeited, I, Child of God awakened in the torment

To behold My Being One with Thee. Pursued I must Be. Be who I AM, One with Thee.

In solitude is comfort, estranged from past yearnings and interests.

I behold my Being, One with Thee.

PUER RESCUES ME

I seek to know my mission and purpose, lest I forget.

The divine child speaks, I – Puer have come to rescue you to perform deeds of wonder.

Albeit, grace. Grace, mystified by the Holy Spirit to embellish the fruits

Of Being: Being One with Thee.

I revel in mystery of my own Being dictated by the sages of antiquity.

Can it be that I AM, My newness prompts (ME)?

I, filled with Love unconditional. I, filled with power and glory.

I, manifested through me by the workings of the Holy Spirit. Amen.

BIRTH OF THE SELF

"The Transcendent Function" (C.G. Jung)

In the recesses of the Soul my spirit wanders discerning the aspects of my Being.

I unencumbered from past yearnings admonish the weakness to be less than I AM.

Behold, I AM brought forth unclaimed, unproclaimed.

The Wind moves: sounds of harmony, bliss, mystery, power and glory spring forth.

Like the Lion on prey, I emerge, shocking to my Soul and yours.

The riches of Solomon exposed in the nakedness of the Self.

GRATITUDE IN MY HEART

I feel gratitude in my heart and being today: a thankful heart for protection

And giftedness, giftedness to be Who I AM. In light of apostasy, weariness

And fatigue beset me. Rest is welcome; hunger fed and satisfied. Albeit

Circumstance granted to be lifted up in the midst of chaos: to be lifted up

And Be Who I AM…ME!

PEACE UNTO MY SOUL

I wake up to my senses, senses of obligation and frustration. Weary of late causes,

I behold. I behold who I AM. Rest when needed. Play when needed. Work at will.

Be not distraught. Peace be unto me, My Soul.

SIMPLICITY OF BEING

Simplicity of Being in the midst of turmoil, in silence. Radiating love embraces the moment Divine Sublime. In juxtaposition. The trees speak to my Soul. The mosquito bites and itching ensues. The fragrance of green, of earth,

Of flower: the bird calls.

MY SOUL SPEAKS

In the recesses of the heart my Being approaches error. Albeit too soon.

Grace granted: manifestation of the One Principle – GOD IS.

Feet encumbered. Walk   Slowly   Steadfast.

I AM ONE WITH MY MAKER

Let me abide in Thee and Thou in ME. I live this principle daily to be the Divine child in expression: manifested Being One with Thee, acclaimed circumstance. To unfold the unique gifts of my God-Being, One with Thee. I unencumbered walk freely with grace bestowed in, through and with ME.

I will to live My Presence through you Divine child of God. All ways, always. Amen.

BREAD OF VICTORY AND SUSTENANCE

The Being: All that is. I Wayfarer continue blessed.

Be it evermore abiding in ME and I in Thee.

The surplus goods of life be stilled to render fruitless.

May the sun/son shine forth this day and all days to bring fruit of Life:

Bread of victory and sustenance. Amen.

PREPONDERANCE OF THE SMALL

Preponderance of the small! What is this I say

When deities foretold a nobler cause, unwavering in light and Being.

I AM. I AM Thee blessed, made whole orchestrated by Divine Principle.

Joy to the Spirit and Soul forthcoming, marked by grace's unfoldment.

Manners and taste reflect the Divine Being: a most gracious state of

Awe, receptivity, creative Being. All is well. Thank You God!

In the silence of my Being I greet Thee. I AM One with Thee.

What makes me falter in direction and going forward?

I am equal. I am even. Liberty knows the Soul of Even.

I know the manna of my heart. My inner stability comes from the God within.

My centered being responds – acts. I can do all things

Through the Christ Who strengthens ME.

YIELD SELF TO SPIRIT'S DESIRE

Jesus has shown us the way to seek Truth. The kingdom is within.

We must go to the Father and in silence hear His message.

Each one of us receives a unique message that pertains to our unfoldment.

We need to continually seek the silence in prayer and meditation to hear the Word.

This gives direction to our lives: purpose and mission.

The process unfolds as we learn to be: that is, be One with the Father.

> Divine Light embrace me
> Divine Light enfold me
> Divine Light show me
> Divine Light lead me
> Divine Light protect me

Divine Light embellish my spirit to be Who I AM. Amen.

I yield myself to Spirit's desire within me.

I seek deliverance of love, light, power, and healing manifested through the Spirit to all of us.

I see Truth to be manifested in Love (content) and Justice (form).

THE TRUE SELF – SON OF GOD

In the context of ME, I AM. I move the sea. I, in the midst of turbulence and fraud, be stilled, and know the I AM.

Behold, I make anew (all things new). The down crest cast, I, suspended in motion AM; bring forth spontaneity – fruit reaped in splendor and array.

I lift mine eyes to the heaven, all Being of Light.

I proceed to propel the images of faith beyond the mundane, to know and Be.

Blessed be me forever: in the far reaches of the divine, the mundane smitten and trampled like the reed in the wind reaching the heights of eternity.

Jesus walking on the water; Jesus calming the waves at sea symbolize our own experience of the divine in the silence. It is in the silence, the point of emptiness where the Divine resides – is, and expresses through the ME a new creation.

This new creation is the fruit of our individuated Self: the true Self, the Divine, Son of God! In being who I AM, I portray the Son of God. I AM my Maker expressed.

The attitude that is thwarting the path of Divine acceptance is being eradicated NOW! Thank You God.

SHOCK TO MY ILLUMINED SOUL

I go before the altar of God, the Soul: the Soul of unquenchable thirst for things divine. I lay before Thee prostrate, giving up myself, my body and my blood to be a vehicle of expression of the Divine Embrace. My path thwarted not, except of my making. I share my gift of healing to the world and universe at large. It is a momentous task: Opening the reservoirs of Dabar to be who I AM. This Divine embrace overshadows all that I do, say and AM. In fleeting moments I linger to be embraced again and again. it matters not where I AM. Encounters bud forth to the chagrin of being One with Thee. This newness, the stranger heretofore is a shock to my illumined SOUL. The fears of yesteryear and now fade into the abyss of nothingness. The channel of divine grace expands beyond the boundaries into the diving imagination to humble myself to let go, be, become the Playmate of divine wisdom. Gifts unlimited, beyond man's hope and dreams. Can it be true?

In our separation misunderstood, I wish to share this; my gift experience with my fellow man. Eros of God: Lamb of God. Amen.

ILLUSORY DETACHMENT

In the recesses of the heart the mind lingers to bestow havoc on the newness of becoming. The emotions erratically persist to be in charge. Awareness of the feelings is initially blocked. Underlying fear captivates all expressions of self-doubt. Emotions run rampant. Unencumbered past bursts forth to free the obstacles of obsession. The transfixed mind explodes in negativity. Gradually, the mind distances itself to look at the feelings. This detachment that develops frees the person to become fully human and alive: the person he/she is meant to be. The explosion of emotion dissipates to nothingness. Then, the person is freed to be who she/he is: the individuated soul. The illusions are no longer adhered to but seen with a bird's eye view. In this manner creativity (Dabar) and love/passion (Eros) harmoniously bring the content (love) and form (justice) into rightful measure in Being. This process is inevitable in each Soul's journey.

YOU AND I ARE THE LIGHT OF THE WORLD

The awe and wonder of my soul proclaims the steadfastness of my Being. I let go of doubts and transgressions harbored long years in vain. Forgiveness is the keynote, to all that is. Being as I AM one with Thee, the unquenchable thirst is quenched. To continue in limitless array, I behold my Maker. The proliferation of greed compels my spirit to pronounce a sentence, a sentence of worth. My sacred Being, whole and well, distorted by perceptions of false making knows you and I – ME are the Light of the World.

EROS COME HOME TO THE SOUL

I go before the holocaust to comfort, to console you and me. Dabar makes known the passionate love of Thy embrace. Now dependent; how empty my vessel: my body and blood prostrate to receive the wealth and riches of Being, Being one with Thee. Eros, unencumbered, beckoned, called to reside in the Soul responds to Life, to grace, to Being. Eros, passion of all passion, splendor of all splendor, magnificent, beholden to Divine Principle, Order, Rule, Justice, Truth, condoned by no One. Eros, come home at last to the soul. Amen.

BE WHO I AM

How humbling it is to Be: be who I AM. Sorrow, let go to Be! Judge not! Love and be loved. Dwell in the mystery of Being, being who I AM: the individuated Self unfolding like the cocoon to the butterfly. Transformed, yes.

> Yes to my spirit; yes to my soul. Yes to your spirit; Yes to your soul.
> I AM. Oneness of Being.

TRUST

I AM: One in Being. Forgetfulness of who I AM creates disturbance in my Being. The moment is paramount. Suffer Me not to succumb to the wishes of the false Self-pride, Vanity, Arrogance, forgetting I can do all. I AM doing all that needs to be done. NOW.

THE JOURNEY OF THE HARVEST

Centering: a centered life, a way of Being is forthcoming with Thy/My making. Circumstances forfeited, fears dispelled, trust, trust, trust, trust. Trust the process. Calm the sea to Be. Be One with Thee/Me.

I AM Passion. I AM the cry in the Wilderness. I AM all that is and ever will Be. Come, my child, succumb to my Blessings bestowed on Thee so bountifully. Bring forth fruit of the Victor. Unfortunate as it may seem, the Truth is known. The grief stricken wayfarer that I AM, I come.

I come through you to bless all, be all, give all; in humility, in greed, in honor, to be who I AM: Son of God, Mother of God, Principle of God, Divine Father of all Life expressed through ME, child of God. Reject not my plea for Life! I call to you my brother and sister to share the journey of the harvest: the Kingdom/Queendom of Heaven on Earth.

UNDERSTANDING EROS

The dawn of Life breaks through. Can Eros be understood more fully? Yes.

I think so. In action. Eros, controlled by the movement of the Soul. Eros springs forth like the lion to devour or savor all in its path. When Eros is invited to come home to the Soul, and stay home, the union creates steadfastness: steadfastness of heart, proliferated by Being one with Thee.

Is it true? I seek to know. I seek to live and breathe and Be One with Thee. Here again, I remind myself of Truth. The Soul knows truth. Eros leads the Truth, only after awakening: that is, coming home to the Soul.

SHARING MY GIFT

I AM celebrating the Divine Light empowered by ME. That ME, the birthed ME, the Puer is the "body of ideas and consciousness of the unfolding process of Life." (Emerson). I dare to love My God not to imitate. I dare to love My God divinely. I dare to be who I AM. My heart is filled with fire to be who I AM. I know. This is my mission, my gift of understanding I share with you, my brother and sister.

I seek Justice in Love. My call, my plea to you is: Let us reason together. Let us end suffering, pain, illusion. Let us be One, Interdependent. This is God's wish. This is my wish. Amen.

OPEN TO THE NEW

I go in unto the altar of God. To God, the Joy of ME. Alleluia. Alleluia.

I enjoy the wake of deliverance: deliverance from error, to light, love and joy of Being. I AM! I AM Thee! Crucified again and again to the dictates of the Soul. I AM One in Being Thee. Amen. The harvest relinquishes past endeavors to open and respond to the new.

HUMILITY GRANTED

I reside within the sanctuary of my Soul. The fears, dispelled of reason proliferate unobtrusively to destroy the makings of my ever present Being.

I unencumbered respond to the blessings of grace. Heretofore, bliss announced in the wealth of Being: Being One with Thee. May it be made known the wishes of the heart: greed encumbrances dispelled by the divine wishes of Being One with Thee. Humility granted to share the burden of defeat to the soul encumbered with grievances and past mistakes.

PASSION OF BEING

I, you, Thee: we are all worthy. Let us proceed to proliferate the greed of Being: being One with Thee. This passion – embrace will save the world from destruction: destructive forces of nuclear blast; destructive forces of self-loathing.

GOD'S JUSTICE

I humbly call to you, my neighbor to respond to the judgment of Being: God's Justice, unwavering in light and love, to bring joy to the soul in Resurrection of body and soul united with Spirit in One Being; interdependent, full of grace and love. Amen.

I AM THE WAY

Again, the Warrior submerged breaks forth to make known the will of the Creator-Divine. Trust the process. Compelled to greed, let us go forth in harmony to devour the good, the satiable. Let us fill/feel our Being with grace.

I make known the wake/way. I come before you. I AM the Way, the Truth the Light, the love of Life. Amen.

I seek refuge in the strength of the Lord. I can do all things through the Christ Who strengthens me.

THE MYSTERY REVEALED TO ALL

An empty vessel to perpetuate to receive is the goal. I AM my Lord and my Maker. Appointed I must be to do the work cut out for me. My work is to be an example of the Christ in action.

I behold deities before me. The embrace is commensurate with my Spirit. I go before the Lord, my guide to greater things. The healing touch reaps Joy of Spirit. I proceed from light to light in light to accomplish the mundane and impossible, made possible by the light of the Holy Spirit. I seek comfort in new ways you teach me. I AM me. I AM me purified and undenounced: undefiled by the worship of ancestry. The beckoning call springs forth like the lion in winter. I beseech my Maker to bear good fruit so the harvest may be full to feed the hungry and the poor. Poor, we all are until the Holy Spirit fills us with the warmth and glow of Life: Life after death, embracing Resurrection of who we are and are becoming, eternally. Amen.

> The what and who of us joined inseparably to do the work of the Master, Jesus Christ, Who has shaped and revealed to us the mysteries of long-standing confusion.

It is paramount in this time that the Mystery be revealed to all. So we can follow in the footsteps:

Thy/My Kingdom come

Thy/My will be done

In Earth as it is in Heaven

Heaven and Earth made One in the Divine light and substance of all that is.

Amen. Thank You God.

PART FIVE
Mary is the Yes to the Glory of the Resurrection.

Resurrection of Eros

THE AWAKENING HEART:
INTELLIGENT WILL-BEING

RECLAIMING AUTHENTICITY

I go before the holocaust to lay bare the facts of my God and Maker. I seek to be: be who I AM and what I AM. The divine light shines through and empowers me, extending to you a greeting of welcome. Welcome to the journey long awaited and forgotten. We rise up together to be One in relationship.

Oh Divine Embrace, I compel you to grant merit and peace to my brother and sister. in disgrace we have long trodden. However, grace bestowed, we honor the sacred in evil/error to be transformed in the light. We, you, I, they, me, all united in One – Interdependent. I AM me extended to be you. Oh Divine Delight, welcome all, welcome home, welcome home to the Soul. Amen. Alleluia.

A STEP BEYOND

Beyond the threshold of experience lies waiting the gifts of Life. Pursue the unknown, embellished in sweet mystery. Hearken ye listener:

"Be still and know that I AM God!" (Ps. 46:10)

Amen! So be it. Alleluia.

BEING ONE WITH ME THEE

The end is a new beginning. Rise up oh Maker-Child of God. I AM one with Thee. Behold, evermore discreet action take place in the midst of turbulence and fraud.

Behold, I rise before the holocaust to redeem; make whole. Granted rich blessing and favor, I, Your humble servant walk in the path of Light. You are a deliverer of ME. I AM the Light of ME. Hold a lamp of my Soul, evermore. Come to the hole in the secret of ME. The Soul is ME, the heart of ME.

The Soul of ME loves the sea of ME. The Soul knows the secret of my heart in light. The Soul knows the seed of my heart in Thee. The sorrow is my sign of health. The Soul knows Me.

Blessed be Me/Thee, unencumbered with mirroring the divine. It is the way of Being: Being one with Me/Thee.

THE SOURCE OF LIFE

You are the SOUL of ME: the Source of Life. You are a sword of liberty. Break the chains of tradition. I AM a Soul initiated in the mysteries of Life. You are the story of I. I AM the ME.

WE ARE ALL ONE IN GOD

This moment of grace – Thank You God for Being. Being that as I may, beholden to a deity – I – rancor fallen beneath the steps of antiquity, I behold my Maker in awe and wonder of the Soul. Be that as it may, I go forward boldly proclaiming the good News: the good News that you and I shall live in grace: unbestowed, proclaimed, given to you and me from the angel sent realms of posterity. Oh! Ah! We are all of the same divination to be blessed; beholden to a deity; grace granted to fill/fulfill Thy/my wishes.

I/You create. Let us create well. Let us create divinely. Let us create in HIS image and likeness. Let us come to understand who we are. We are One. We are all One in God: Thy/my Maker. Thank You God. Alleluia. Alleluia.

I AM

Here it is, another year, another day to behold my Maker: one with Thee. Amen. I go before the holocaust to blaspheme no one; but to lift up my spirit to announce, denounce no one. All is one in Thee.

Thank You God, for my being one with Thee. Amen. Alleluia. Alleluia. Alleluia. A daily reminder, encounter to remain the steadfast Wayfarer. I search not; beseech not. I AM. Amen.

THE I IS A WINDOW TO THE SOUL

The I is a window to the SOUL. Look beyond the bread you eat. Look beyond the clothes you wear. You are ME, the divine embrace in expression. Go forth to all nations and speak the words of Peace:

Emmanuel, Yahweh, Allah, Aba, Jehovah, Krishna, Father

Thank You for the abundance: abundance of Being one in Thee.

ME

Time will tell the blessings of foreboding Truth: to tell the truth in one word. BE. BE – the paradox of all action, grants grace to be bestowed bounteously. Favor rest in the blessings to respond to grace; thy Maker, amplified by wisdom to withhold judgment of Being.

RELEASING THE BAGGAGE

My soul pronounces a decree. To be less the I AM is not the work of mayhem. It is a response to life-LIFE. It is fitting to behold my being one with Thee. I seek to counter blessings: fruit of wakefulness, fruit of the vine. Conflicts (grim and farcical) engaged in eradicating the lessons of posterity. But the Soul knows truth, and will come to the rescue to make known what needs to be done. You will have a heyday when the awakened ones can see the light of being one in Thee. Make a commitment of choice to BE. Be filled with light to bless the present state of affairs, to learn the lessons God has sent Thee to fulfill thy mission. Thank You God.

Grace forthcoming when I release this baggage that holds me in bondage.

Amen. Thank You God.

THE GRACE OF NO BOUNDARIES

Lest I forget who I AM I bear witness to the fact: All is well in the midst of turbulence and fraud. The grace of no boundaries operates fully unbeseeched by you – me – I. It is the plan, the divine plan of action. Regardless of man's undertaking, posterity's decree will be filled/fulfilled.

VIOLATION OF THE SELF

When time is not taken to be with ME, when time is foregone to BE, we fool ourselves into thinking we have done what is right and just. The anger of the Soul will not tolerate hypocrisy. Repercussions far and wide reaching out into the universe squelch the real ME.

Silence: a must BE, don't fool yourselves. The demons come sevenfold when we squelch the real ME. Discernment is the key. A prayer of supplication I will make to protect my being:

> Dear God, I behold a deity within my Being: Being one with Thee.
>
> Make known the path, make known the way to stay on track and Be Who I AM.

Anger besets me. Moment to moment I must Be who I AM. I bequeath a miracle to be less than I AM is preposterous. Preponderant ways interfere with the blessing of Being. I must forsake the old and grab hold, gravitate to the new. It is a momentous task when one is flanked mercilessly by the gridiron of defeat. I seek to mind my ways to become less stern to squelch the desire to be Who I AM. Exhausted, defeated, I rise up again to be who I AM.

THE CENTER OF BEINGNESS

I still am not at peace warring inside to be who I AM. I make claims to no one. It is paramount: grace unencumbered, come forth. Display your fruitage in abundance. I have needs, genuine. My soul cries out for revenge when stifled, neglected, ignored. Who or what will grant rest or peace from bondage inflicted within and without? I need space and time for expression: expression of the Self manifested from the Divine Center of Love made manifold through countless effort, freed to be at last come home to the Soul. I wandered aimlessly amid the torment of pestilence. Fraud, greed, ignorance, intolerance beseech a vexed spirit. Love abounds in the cool, calm depths of Being: Being one in Thee. Volcanic eruptions dissipate in the center of Beingness. I the victor beseech no more; but go on in the moment to live fully acclaimed with the descent of the Holy Spirit upon ME.

LETTING GO

Time is of the essence in my Being. I the Wayfarer have need of space and quiet. Fatigue makes difficult the Way. Rest, a needed necessity to fulfill my destiny, my Being. Let go of unneeded luxuries. Let go of posterities. Let go of all that is not conducive to the moment of Being; Being one with Thee. Fretful as it may seem, it is the path that leads to enlightenment of Being, Being one in Thee. My mind gets tangled in too much clutter. How do I strip; make simple the task? The Way is. Solitude. Not mine, but Thine. It is the way of the warrior to fight off obscenities. Let be and grow. Grow in light and love and Be. Be whom Thou art in each moment. Each moment of grace compels me to join the wellspring of Life and Be. Be who I AM. Amen. So be it. Alleluia.

BELIEVE IN ME

Come Holy Spirit, fill me with the light of understanding.

I come before the holocaust to make known Thou art a child of God; sincere in endeavoring to do what is right. Make bold pronouncements of what is Truth. Truth laden with guilt is festering weaknesses beyond doubt and transgressions. Make amends. Believe in ME. Drifting to and fro won't do. Be firm. Believe in yourself. Confidence beckons sincerity. Thou art what thou must be. Go. Do. Be blameless.

THE NEED FOR PREPARATION

Lest I confuse the Wayfarer, let Me prepare you for this journey. You will need to be prepared.

Go forth humbly and serve the Lord. Admonish not the sinner. Be content to be. Be whom Thou art. Boldly face and tread this Path, the path of unknowing. Live moment to moment awake to all life. Non-judgment is the key. Blessed be each and all in Christ. Amen.

BE BLAMELESS

Speak Lord. I'm listening.

Behold Thee, Son of God

Unworthy, worthy to be distraught to seek amends on thy behalf. Blow out the candle of desire to be less than I AM. I beseech Thee to make known the fruit of the Vine. Behold! I AM Thee with you and in you. Go forth. Proclaim the good news. I AM one with my Maker.

In illumining myself, I illuminate others.

Your job is to be. Be whom Thou art: the sole purpose of existence for Thee in ME. Go forth. Bud. Bloom. Grow into the rose, the lily – in fullness of Being. That is your job. Fret no more. Be Love. Do. Be Blameless. The ferment of seasoning takes hold swiftly when one can see/be/live simply, abundantly in grace. You, who are mother and child, bride and bridegroom: Go. BE. Love. Do blamelessly. Always fearing does not produce the Kingdom.

Thy Kingdom come. Thy/My will be done.

In the quiet stillness of my heart, I abide in Thee and Thou in Me. I make known the path, the endless journey, abounding in principle, to behold who I AM. Thank You God. Amen.

I AM ONE WITH THEE IN PRINCIPLE AND GRACE

Come Holy Spirit, fill my cup with vintage wine. O Lord, heal me in your splendor. I have loved Thee/me: the son of Thy Being.

I AM one with Thee in principle: not only in principle but in grace, grace in Thy openness to one, oneness in Being. Thank You my God. My glory is pronounced with favor to Thy glorious resurrection and Being. Now there is one Son. I AM with Thee. Thanks be to God, Amen. Alleluia.

Thank you God for your bounteous glory. This day do I seek to make new; renew the face of the earth within me. I go before the holocaust and proclaim LOVE abounding: grace, ever present to behold my Maker, forgiving each moment of discontent. Make known the path of love and light ever reaching to the ends of the Earth. I seek old wine to restore and make new wineskins, and fill with new wine: each moment of grace, each moment of love, each moment of peace. Amen. Justice reigns ever glorious in Thy/my presence. Truth abides in Me forever. Thank you God. Alleluia.

A NEW REGIME

We linger on the past because we have not lived in the fullness of time. Our hearts are mellowed in the process of becoming. Sorrow conditions us to Be. The onlooker's choice is ever present. We have to be who we are. When we are, we manifest the Christ principle. The Cosmic assurance will not let us down or deceive us. The light: the enlightened Beingness propels us to proper action foretold in the resurrected Spirit of Jesus.

I come to you, I claim to you a new regime, blessed and holy for all mankind. No plunder or pestilence, no deceit or laughter mocking, I the Spirit of all ages: holy, divine, endowed everlasting, glorious, glorified in Beingness.

I, the Wayfarer, beseech you and me to listen, to respond to the kingdom-grace, bounteous, overflowing to lift us up to humanhood: Human-Divine; our rightful heritage and blessing. God love us. May we love God, and respond to the notion of posterity.

Pestilence forsaken, hardships foregone; suffer no more My children. Be whom thou art; the divine Love, Wisdom, Truth in expression for all ages to come, for posterity. Amen. So be it. Alleluia. Praise and thanksgiving forever.

The new heaven and the new earth manifested in our Beingness, propelled in expression in the mirror of light and love are here to stay embodying the divine, sublime. We are all One in relationship; interdependent. So be it. Amen. Alleluia.

RESURRECTION IS ON THE THRESHOLD OF EXISTENCE

Thank you God for this bounteous glorious day. Resurrection is on the threshold of life, of existence. Beware the falsification of past endeavors to behold Thy Son, ever bounteous and full reigning in glory.

Circumstance, propelling desire to limits beyond the threshold of reason, gratuitous mistakes accompany any great undertaking. Be it for man or God or both.

Tumultuous, glorious, ever reigning, blessed in grace, love. Undertaking the momentous task of Thy brethren, the sheep flock in false alarm. A backlist of events propel the visitor to circumspect. Accountable, yes. Reason, no. A God forsaken forsakes not the path. He is bent to follow. Narrow it must be to acclaim the acceptance of the masses.

Your duty is to your Self: the God-deity bestowed upon. The grace of no boundaries propel the masses to circumspect: delivered from obscenity, delivered to love, light, wisdom, glory; ever glorious, far reaching into the abyss of hell to the heaven's sent glory of resurrection and ascensions to fulfill destiny.

RESENTMENT AGAINST THE ESTABLISHMENT OF BEING

My heart harbors resentment against the establishment of Being. How can this be? It must be true. Therefore, I seek purification of the heart. Mary, Queen of Life, I pray to you for deliverance: deliverance of the message of will-being. My soul, preponderant in its ways, needs the Spirit to refresh and renew Me. If my soul responds properly, I will magnify the Lord and I will be joy-filled.

I AM the Spirit of my Maker. Rejoice and be glad: fruit of the vine. The purification of the heart is a noble task unbeknown and hidden to the Wayfarer. The mystery of myself continues to unfold.

RESPONSE TO JUSTICE IN TERRORISM: CONVERSION

I have drunk the wine of my ancestors. Even Jesus has done so. I bewildered, search for truth and meaning regarding the present state of affairs. How do I respond in justice to terrorism? Forgiving? Yes. But what is the action of society that is needed? Conversion.

Conversion: Scientific Example

H_2O = two parts hydrogen to one part oxygen = WATER

The mirroring in nature is a reflection of our own conversion. In this process/change, we become new; a complete being of power anointed by the Holy Spirit. It is our destiny to become the integral aspect/being, human/divine, coupled with elaborate testimony made prevalent by the massacre of man.

"My God, My God, why have You forsaken me?"

This total abandonment, sacrifice if you will, is the result of decay of man's integral wellspring of initiation into the mystery of the Resurrection: the life-giving principle of all Being. (Mary is the Yes to the glory of the Resurrection.)

The wellsprings of imagination feed my soul to respond to the call of my Maker. I in justice seek to proclaim a new regime.

"Blessed are the peacemakers for they shall inherit the Earth." This means peace within thine own self to respond to peace within thine own brother and sister.

THE SOUL'S WOUNDING: DISTRACTIONS

My whole being is disturbed and in grief. The soul has been deprived again by distractions that hurt the soul. The soul needs balance: work, play, friends, beauty, love, truth. The trickery, the evil comes in disguise, in dress if you will, undiscerned by the Wayfarer. This repeated distracted way of living and responding to the moment is devastating to the soul. The heart, unbeknown to the detriment of the soul, is the lure for the corrupted past and present state of affairs. Get thee behind me Satan, is a moment-to-moment encounter.

The advanced soul can also get caught in this trap. The lack of peace, emptiness, that hole in the heart feeling is a readable sign that something is going on; that something is birthing in the soul. The mystery of Being is self-propelled. Creative endeavors erupt and bloom. The God within beholds me to be who I AM.

RESTORATION OF MEMORIES

I decried my spirit for revenge: revenge of the soul. Meek and humble as it is, it still persists in old patterns; wants to take hold, defaulting in Being. It is cantankerous to say the least. I will be nourished in magnificence only when I am able, free to be who I AM. It is paramount to give credence to old ways of Being; manifesting the desire, but not the commitment. Commitment: insist, have. Or no use is posterities decree to grant me refuge and strength to be who I AM.

I love the quiet stillness. I love the awe and splendor. I love Being. But traps are beckoning moment to moment: judgment, criticism, reason. Intellect's habits pursue advantages unknown to spirit and soul. The wine of my ancestors speak fruitfully; less I disparage this grace to be less than I AM.

I love the Me. Move on to new horizons now to bequeath what is readily unknown. I have been blessed: riches amply stored in the labyrinths of my soul. I drink the wine to restore the memories of long forgotten past. It is my destiny to share with the brethren, receptive or not. It is my duty to proclaim. I must not alter or falter on the course. Judgments left by me, intellect forsaken, I bequeath what is real in this moment of everlasting Truth. I have been given the space, the time, the ample rewards of perseverance through faith: blind though it was in infancy, of impregnated bliss foretold in the glory of the resurrection and assumption of spirit and body of Mary, Queen of us all.

RESPOND AND CLAIM THE GRACE OF NO BOUNDARIES

Mary, Queen of the May, I/We glorify thy Being, thy commitment, thy response to thy Maker. Behold You/Thee ever glorious, glorified and redeemed through the suffering and agony of Jesus, your son, our teacher and brother. Thank you for being You; true to your mission, your destiny, your call. May we respond and claim the grace of no boundaries to fulfill our purpose and our mission. Thank you for showing us the way home by your example.

May you be exalted this day, this month in the heavens and in the earth. This is my decree, my tribute; woman to woman, human to human-divine sublime, all-being in Christ resurrected glorious forevermore. Thank you. Thank you. Thank you. My humble and prostrate offering of the soul; my soul, all souls, Mother Earth. May you reign glorious, undisturbed by man's obstinacy, hardness of heart. Posterities decrees fulfilled, blessed in all-Beingness, may I likewise respond and in humble awakenings respond to the call of my Maker; the call through your glorious Resurrection and Assumption into heaven.

PURIFICATION OF THE HEART

O Beloved in strength, you are the relevant aspect of Being in ME. I forsake the ME to be purified: purified in the heart. Mary, Queen of the May, thank you for responding to my call for purification of the heart. Amen. Thank you God. So be it. Amen. Alleluia. Alleluia. Alleluia.

RESPOND TO THE GRACE OF NO BOUNDARIES

I committed to be who I AM; I in spite of exhaustion continue, the magnitude the awe, the splendor of grace; the limitless boundaries of the soul in the spirit and love of Jesus, the Christ. How can I share the fruitage of the vine? Trust! Trust! Trust! It is paramount in this time and place to be who I AM. It is I, fruit of the vine responding to grace; the grace of no boundaries to the soul.

INSTRUCT TO CHOOSE THE PATH OF SAVING GRACE

My people perish on the wrong path, the path to destruction. Instruct to choose the path of saving grace. The Holy Grail is a wisdom ages old to respond to. We, immortal need to be cognizant of our choice. Free will makes paramount this decree: the blood of Jesus the Christ crucified through me again and again. How can this be? I inherit through faith and commitment to be example of my Maker, the Father in heaven through the most Holy Spirit expressed through Jesus the Christ now. Through me the Christ supreme withstands all judgment and decrees. It no longer is the burden of the me! It includes the burden and salvation and light of all the brethren. Amen. So be it. Alleluia.

THE BIRTH OF ME IS THE TRUE BEGINNING

No! The birth of Me is not the point of rest. It is the true beginning; the beginning to release and be the I AM. I, floundering, unprotected by a mentor, only the Holy Family: Jesus, Mary, Joseph Me to be who I AM. Why Me? It is the foreboding Truth. Openness to grace. It pours in bounteously, unlimited. I the humble Wayfarer respond as best I can. I the empty vessel prostrate before Thee, my God, my Maker! I AM the wholesome Me. I search the labyrinths of my soul to be propelled in manifestation: manifestation of the Holy Spirit. I, one with my Maker must respond to the call of reason: reason to be together, unblemished in principle and desire.

WELCOME HOME TO THE HEART PURIFIED

Free will is the culprit, the key: the key to be who I AM. The sloth of past enterprise terminated by the understanding and foreboding Truth of the responsibility of man: responsibility to respond to truth: the truth of helplessness in the sight of the Lord. helpless I AM in the face of anger, fear, in short, the seven deadly sins. if I be lifted up in grace, then posterities communion and balance restore the necessary ingredient for the salvation of man: desire, willingness to persevere through the torrential fires and rain of the aggravated self, depleted in Beingness in ages past.

Now is the time, this moment of grace to bestow on Thy brethren a welcoming home, home to the heart; purified, divine, sublime in the works of mercy of the Holy Family: Jesus, Mary, and Joseph. I decree a blessing. I pronounce a commitment for all to respond to the call elevating and restoring the human-divine relationship. Amen. Thank you God. Alleluia! Alleluia! Alleluia!

I still in awe, moment to moment. I Me You We All of us One. I humbly accept my purpose and mission to share my gift of understanding through the prophetic call and anointing of the Holy Spirit. Amen.

THE GLORY OF RESURRECTION

Vulnerable I am. From new life, I move to death. The anointing of the Holy Spirit propels me to the brink of insanity. Why? Because of long forgotten past, the Truth! Truth and reality, a mixed blessing forfeits the desire to be less than I AM. Preponderant ways interfere with this expedition of awe and wonder. The labyrinths of my soul search out meaningfulness. Sloth, a demon of my own making rises up. Resistance to being joy-filled is the culprit. But I, if I be lifted up in grace, the grace of no boundaries, trust will bring the change. Change of the heart, purified, sublime does wonders for the soul. Now the soul can continually respond to NEW LIFE. Amen. Alleluia. Thank you Mary, Mother of God. The glory of Resurrection is upon Me, manifested through the Holy Spirit, the divine spark within. Amen. So be it. Alleluia.

You, God know all my needs, be they cumbersome or light. You know my sad heart that needs transformation in love and light. I ask the Holy Spirit to respond to my slothful way. I pray that I, masking the shadow of even will display the fruitage of the vine. Heretofore, be it my favor and blessing to let go; erase sloth and express the joy-filled Resurrection of my Being. Amen.

The home stands on its own. I stand on the Rock of Christ. I seek to mind my ways. I will be Thy presence, O God! It is the I in You that I contemplate. It is the I in me that is the witness-bearing Truth of all Being.

I AM my soul and my obliterated by the sea of divine light. I AM Me.

DEAR GOD

Dear God,

I am seeking your power and wisdom and strength to orchestrate my thoughts, words, actions: my very Being. Amen.

Look to the sources of antiquity. Go beyond the mundane. View the world at large. The scope of your enterprise reaches far beyond the elements of elementary being.

My heart favors resentment that never was or will be. Resentment dissipates to its nothingness in the presence of Thy/My Being; Whither shall I go in the midst of tribulation? The wolves howl at my door.

In the recesses of your/my heart, your/my very being speaks. It is here that we commune in our solitude to strengthen and uplift the self and the world.

I go before the holocaust and proclaim a new world of victory: victory to be who I AM. Amen.

ADHERENCE TO THE LAW OF FAITH

I fatigued, come before you, my God.

All is well. Be not afraid.

To mirror the divine Christ light requires adherence to the law of Faith. What is the Law of Faith?

To believe and receive one and the same in honest, pure intention of the heart. The soul dies to all carnal desire, knowledge, will. The soul in resurrected state of being is one with the Father. Eros come home to the soul-disciplined is the beginning of a New Regime. If man's understanding be awakened, he will respond to the call of his Maker. Unbeknown to him, the process is going on toward fulfillment. However, much suffering can be alleviated by the fuller cooperation of man. Long-standing grievances need to be dealt with for all mankind. The grievance of separation is no small matter. It is paramount in this time to seek recompense for past mistaken endeavors.

I go before the Father undisclosed to bring into alignment my thinking heart: Thy/My will be done. Amen.

I COMMAND A NEW REGIME

In the deep reservoirs of my Being, I command a New Regime. Posterities dilemma obliterated, I AM Me unproclaimed, justified through the Christ. While it is the way of angels, the brethren walk in light. Heretofore, my Being has been a stamp of grace. Now my Being is obliterated by the divine sense of worship: Presence Power Glory made manifest through long endured suffering to be less than I AM. It is time to propel the masses in a new state of Being: Being for lifted from the immersion in the deadly state of affairs, lifted to the inner most depths of the soul to commune with God, my Maker.

> Our Father Who art Me
>
> Hallowed be Thee/Me
>
> Hallowed be Me/Thee

Once and for all, recognition of Truth sets us on a path heretofore unproclaimed. This new way of being is paramount to uplift the whole human race. Mankind is on the precipice of reason to be lifted up to his calling in grace. May we join in the communion of Saints, the resurrection of the body and life everlasting.

In the depths of my soul I wander to proclaim, what of Satan, Lucifer, this entity bigger than life that surrounds and controls the obstinate. He is a false god, set apart and rejected by many. But I say unto you, love your enemy. Be not afraid. The enemy within is transformed through desire of the heart, through openness to grace, through response to my mentor, the Christ. All is well. The nations crumble. Posterities decree lives on. Eros, transformed in the light and love is the blessing of grace, grace freely bestowed. The only requirement is opening the heart to receive. Amen. Awakening intelligent Being. Thanks be to God. Alleluia. Alleluia. Alleluia.

RESPOND TO THE MOMENT IN GRACE

The call of my Maker prompts me to respond to the moment in grace: grace bestowed so bounteously to be who I AM. I take this moment to share this experience of grace. The light shines forth when I AM willing to respond. The helpless soul needs direction/steering. The me is encumbered. The human divine call lifts us beyond the precipice of reason. I no longer am content to be less than I AM. I break all the rules of daily existence. Society's lies/ignorance cannot be tolerated by the enlightened ME. The passion of desire breaks forth. This communion, passion of desire is necessary for my Being. I AM becoming wholly other. This obligation gives credence to my Soul to respond in humility and grace. I question the wisdom of my undertakings – sanding, painting, cutting grass.

These are contemplative experiences to be honored as worthwhile and sacred. Do not be concerned with the end result. Trust. Remember, trust the process. The house mirrors your own Soul that you/I are now working on. Belief in the Resurrection is enough. Trust. Faith will set you clear of all obstacles. Remember Mary's faith. Respond likewise. Behold! I make all things new.

Thank You God. I now leave. I go to paint the house in preparation: preparation for the Glorious Resurrection: celebration of thine own Beingness. Yes! It is time. The fruit of the vine is ripe. Amen. Alleluia. Thank You God. I must go to take my leave to paint NOW. With grace operative moment to moment, I can accomplish all things.

BEING ONE WITH THEE

Behold! I make all things new. Amen. You are Jesus, the Son of ME now. The Son of ME is Jesus. How can this be? Being one with the Father is the Son of ME.

In the recesses of the heart I search my Soul: Soul unencumbered
with grace, grace bestowed abundantly to the Wayfarer.

"What you do to the least of my brethren, you do unto ME!"

I AM. I seek wholeness, harmony in being, Being One with Thee.
In response to Life, Yahweh my God is the messenger of my Soul.
In the darkness I let go and respond to being, Being One with Thee.

Oh come to Me My people; Respond to the Joy of Resurrection.
Open Thy loins and gird Thy strength to respond to the NEW.
I AM with Thee all times, all ways! Amen.

Oh Israel! Are we to repeat Thy vain response,
Crucifying our children in utter contempt?
Respond to our plea in the darkness. This dark hour.
Your/My/Our cries in the wilderness go on.

Despair now My children, but make your ways My way.
In the comforts of My bosom I nurture and feed you.

THE SOUL'S NEED: THE JOY TO BE

I awake to my soul's need: the joy to be.
I, plagued no longer with ills
The ripe mellowing of fruited wine from the vine. I AM.

Blest be my soul and all of life. Heretofore, I go in peace to welcome
The beggar, the traveler, the displaced. Have mercy on thine own self.
Frustrations and hatreds laid aside, come to the harvest. Welcome.

My soul responds to a greater calling, calling to be Who I AM.
I floundered long in vain hopes, but now rejoice in Thy/My Being.
It has been an arduous Journey. The fight with Self is War.
STOP! Take heed. Rest awhile. Commingle with Being.

The baggage has to go or I (the God within) will be destroyed.
I pray for deliverance of this baggage. This "evil" in worldly understanding
Has to go or I can't be ME.
I pray for release of the bondage, this enslavement NOW!

INSTRUCTION

Be a light to the soul. Eros is moving, moving in a new way to a new Place.
Let this mystery be forthcoming in my Being.
I seek Your will in being a light to the Soul.
Eros is the heel of the 'No Man.'

We can stop at the point of Resurrection of Being and choose not to go further.
We choose. What is the intention of the Heart?

>Our God, Father and Mother
>
>>You restore us
>>You fulfill us
>>You instill us
>>You make us whole.

TAKE TIME TO PRAISE THE SOUL IN ME

When do I take time to praise the soul in ME?
    Glory to the Soul. Glory   Glory   Glory
Glory to the Soul for All days to come. Beseech Thee no more.
Make manifest the Works of Mercy: Feed the hungry! Clothe the naked!
    Respond to the call of Thy Maker.

The harvest depends on Thy/My willingness to respond to the gifts of posterity.

    My soul magnifies the Lord
    My spirit rejoices in Thee. (Luke 1:46 & 47)

Overwhelmed with joy, I beseech no more but go on to deliver the message
Of the fruit of the vine. Alleluia Alleluia Alleluia!
In the wake of the forest I bequeath my spirit to rescue the Once forgotten Truth
To be delivered to the brethren raised up and glorified forevermore.
Thy grace abounds for all in all through all. Amen. So be it. Alleluia!

My soul once weary and old has rejuvenated to the blessings of posterity.
Thank You My Lord, My God, My Maker. Alleluia Alleluia Alleluia.
Glory and Being forevermore. Amen Amen Amen.

The harvest of the labor responds to the Joy of Resurrection.
The secret flower opens to respond to the new.
Blasphemed by No One, it is fortuitous blessings of ages past.
Be One! Live One with My God, My Maker.

FAITH WITHOUT WORKS IS DEAD

If believing and receiving with honest, pure intention of the heart describes what is meant by the Law of Faith, we have some deep considerations to ponder.

The faith experience presupposes an admonition to truth of being, being one with Thee, my God and Maker. I succumb to the profound blessings of truth to receive the divine works of mercy in operation: in experience, in life.

True work begins with the self and is resurrected in Being. To admonish the sinner means to look at oneself, to love the weakness but not support that weakness. 'I can do all thing through the Christ who strengthens me.'

The experience of faith, <u>true faith</u> is the resurrection of beingness, being one with Thee, the divine. Heart, spirit and soul are united harmoniously without the push/pull of dualities bombarding at/in each moment. This is a momentous leap from the standpoint of our human experience, intellect – if you will. It requires living in each moment with that divine presence consciously, inescapably grounded in our very being-existing life. Each cell in the body is permeated with this presence in a powerful way.

This type of being/awareness is truly and surely expressed in the world in which we live. Mother Theresa and Father Bede Griffeth (recently deceased) are perhaps the best examples displaying the fruitage of the vine. Thanks be to God. Amen.

RECEIVE THE RESURRECTED LAMB

Amazing Grace Melody

The moon is wan, the son is light
The bough is bent to receive.
I know the I AM, that I-eye AM
The light of love received.

Redeemed in the night of Love
Behold my Soul relieved.
In bliss foretold, in dying receive
The Resurrected Lamb.

I AM the light in ME.
I AM the Love in ME.
I AM the Soul of ME.
I AM the Soul in me.

THE CALL FROM THE UNIVERSE

I seek to respond to the divine calling today. Grant me the openness and wisdom to respond to Thy Grace. Amen.

Heart, spirit and soul united, joined as one, rejuvenated in the wake of understanding: my bliss comes from being. My torment comes from beseeching in wrong endeavors of spirit and soul. The wake of understanding beckons me to respond to grace. Thy/My will be done. Compassion of the heart makes me Stop! Look! Listen! Grace forthcoming bestows all blessing.

Grant me the wisdom to follow through and respond to Your blessing. Amen.

I have a special calling from the universe to open the seal of wealth and riches of posterity.

The divine light and wisdom shine through Me. I pray that I be a fitting instrument of Thy will. Amen.

The reservoirs of Dabar are opened/opening NOW!

I succumb to the blessings of truth and worship. Amen.

My soul has felt so angered and wounded.

> Come, Holy Spirit lift up my heart, my very self to understand the meaning of this experience.

AWAKEN MY HEART TO THE NEW

I behold a deity festered in grief, stricken to oblivion,
Behold to reach for blessings, blessings bestowed to bounteously
To awaken the dead soul.

The heart encumbered in breached contract expels the varmint of worms.
In so doing, the grieving process ensues.
And sadness stricken, the dilemma foretold foretells a new way.
Death of the old makes way for the new.
My bared emotions show no gain, but are rent with grief asunder.
When I have expelled the varmint of worms
I renewed in hope and grace will comply to the standards of posterity.
The standards foretell a new way.
May I be open to grace to receive the bountiful harvest.

THE DIVINE WORKS OF MERCY

If we ask the right questions, perhaps we can reach a starting point to make the world a better place in which to live.
What are the divine works of mercy?
Forgiveness
Repentance
Compassion
Command Eros to come home, stay home in the Soul
Resurrection of Eros
No to continuance in ignorance!
FAITH is ears of the SOUL
LOVE is the ears of the HEART
HOPE is the light of the SOUL.

REAL CHANGE

In pondering the question of me, I seek to discover who am I.

The I is the divine at works in mercy.
I AM reflects the being of Posterity.
I seek new wine in/for new wine skins in seeking to replenish/restore the old in wholesome order.

The chaos of question muddles the mind. Doubts and transgressions lift the mind to a new order of being: being far removed from the divine sense of worship of posterity. Separation of the self from the elements of Being is devastating/preposterous for the Soul.

The Soul needs comforts, assurances. Tepid faith is not conducive to the wellsprings of the heart response. An all-out effort needs to be made to stimulate the primal instincts of nature. That is, man needs to control the aspects of reason that interfere with the groundedness of Being.

Creativity has gone out on a limb so to speak. We need to seriously question: What are we creating in violence, in hopelessness, in despair, in aggravated assault, in extraordinary means to sustain life in a body with a dead Soul?

The mongrel of competition doesn't evoke the natural sense of wonder and awe in Being. How do we change a world so bent on destructive a course?

Population explosion continues without the necessary wholesome upbringing of our youth. We live what we learn.

It is time to take a backward glance at history. Violence begets violence. Love begets love. The unending struggles continue until we wake up and change.

> "Where you put love in,
> You draw love out."   — St. John of the Cross

Real change begins with the divine works of mercy in operation. These are:

> Forgiveness   Repentance   Compassion

Justice and Truth are the wellsprings of imagination for a New Regime. Justice and Truth are operative only in the context of forgiveness, repentance and compassion concomitantly.

Let us renew our faith and open up the wellsprings of imagination to incorporate the sublime. In awe and wonder and gratitude I seek to fulfill the prophecies of old. Amen. Thanks be to God.

THE DIVINE SONSHIP

To understand the Soul, we have to understand the basis of culture. The divine essence of Being incorporates the Soul. The magnificence of the soul is postulated according to the Gospel of Luke.

"My soul doth magnify the Lord..."   Luke 1:46

The soul is the malleable aspect of Being open to suggestion. It is the creative receptor for spirit. The discipline of the soul determines our ability to respond to the message of the Gospel.

Our Father Who art in heaven
Hallowed be Thy name
Thy Kingdom come
Thy will be done
On Earth as it is in Heaven
Give us this day our daily bread
And forgive us our trespasses
As we forgive those
Who trespass against us
And lead us not into temptation
But deliver us from evil. Amen.

The discipline of the soul presupposes obedience to the Father in heaven. This includes adherence to the laws of the Universe. Since Genesis 3, we have been the disobedient servant. It is not an easy matter to go back to the purity and perfection of the first man, Adam. What is required?

First: Opening the Heart

Remember Jesus tells us of the hardened heart. The heart has to be opened for the soul to respond as receptor of the divine. Therefore, forgiveness and repentance are the first step to recovery of a lost generation of perfect harmony with God. Jesus came to show and teach us this lesson. He offered His body and blood to allow our passage into the divine receptacle of being. This is what is meant by. "By Your cross and Resurrection You have redeemed the World." It establishes the hope, once and for all: The <u>Divine Sonship</u>. Let us respond to this lesson of posterity with heartfelt gladness and thankfulness. Amen.

MAY I IN BREACHED CONTRACT BE FORGIVEN

I come as a brother concomitant in grief

To behold my Maker, sublime and divine

In awe and wonder, I grace the Universe.

Behold my destiny, my feat forfeited by clutter

Clutter – inner and outer

My heart saddened, grief stricken to behold such insanity.

Oh Holy Spirit, gracious One, come to my aid to renew my hope in me,

In humanity. Amen.

I seek order in my life to fulfill destiny. May I, in breached contract be forgiven. And forgive, now and for all posterity, Amen. So be it. It is done. Thanks be to God.

The wellsprings of imagination feed my Soul. My Soul so bounteously forgiven and bestowed upon: the works of mercy from the divine embrace of the God within.

I go before the holocaust and now lay to rest the divine work of mercy to renew faith and hope, the wellsprings of Love – encountered blessings. Amen.

Follow Me. Love Me. You owe a seed of Love.

I seek to begin anew with Peace (end warring and conflict – inner and outer).

My tortured soul continues in anger and unrest: obstacles forthcoming from the inner recesses of the heart, the heart poisoned by the selfish greed of past enterprise. I ask my Higher Self to conform and release the pressures of obstinacy provoking thought, waywardness, rebellion.

I seek to know my inner most Being to harmonize with the beauty of nature

And all that is.

I AM One with Thee my God

I seek to be Me. Release Me.

This also means: I can't have others dictating this ME, only the God within Through Jesus the Christ, Resurrected and Savior. I wish to receive my King. I wish my heart to prepare room for the Christ. Let Heaven and Nature sing through Me/me, with Me/me, in ME/me. Amen. So be it. Thank You God.

In the cloister of my Being, I propel the masses. It is time to register the proof of my convictions.

PURITY OF THE HEART

Come Holy Spirit, enthrall me with your grace to bestow bounteously on the brethren, so they too will reap the benefits of Thine utter simplicity of/in Love.

I commend you, beseech you to win favor in Thy/my blessings.

It is no use if I in greed, corruption seek Thine/mine. Purity of heart dispels all need of misfortunate vanities. What are the conditions or state of Purity in Heart? Purity means spotless, without a trace of malice or greed self-serving. Sublimation of the will to the Father is essential, all encompassing. The ego receives direction/instruction from the Father through the Holy Spirit. Discernment of spirit is self-enticing. I come to You/Thee in abandonment: abandonment of all self-sacrificing attitude and whim and supplant a thankful joyful heart of receptivity to the Divine Creator of all that is and will be. Amen.

Yes, now is the time to trust. And I, weak in trust and supplant my greed to be open: receptor of Your will in trust. Fear does not aid my countenance. I respond now to the Law of Faith to believe and receive with honest pure intention of the heart.

May the Holy Spirit shower upon me the honesty to receive Thee in trust. Amen. Thanks be to God.

PART SIX

A thankful joyful heart is receptor of the divine creator of light and wisdom.

The gift of the Christ the new born

THE AWAKENED HEART: INTELLIGENT ONE

PURE IN HEART

I respond to my mentor, the Christ. How do I fit in? I am me unjustified. I behold my Maker. In wonder and awe, I proclaim a new day. May it be fitting to be who I AM. Bless my spirits. Behold my Maker, my Being. In the throes of darkness and torment, I beseech no more. I AM filled with the light of the Christ. I go before the brethren uncondemning, freed to be at last, one and whole in my Being. Amen. Thank You God.

The feminine principle developed, developing to behold my Maker, my Being, Mother of even, transcendence of opposites. If I become one and the same with my Maker, the light shines through at any given moment. I go on in discourse. The end is near in hard labor. Delivery-deliverance of the word in bodily form, manifestation makes easy, simple the task to be Who I AM. Trust, the hope in the heart, purified, sublime. I no longer have needs unmet. Mary, Queen of us all responds in due time to alleviate our weaknesses with our cooperation: in strength, in obligation, in wisdom, in futility ended. This is a new way of Being grasped by the Pure in Heart. Amen. So be it. Alleluia.

A BREAKDOWN OF TRINITARIAN THOUGHT

FATHER	MOTHER	SON	HOLY SPIRIT
SPIRIT	matter	indwelling self	overshadows Mother
Creator	forgive	Christ principle	Mother aspect
Indweller	compassion	One	
Manifest	heal	Intelligent Soul	
infinite consciousness	unconditional love	Reveals	
WISDOM	evenness		
Reason	purity	meditates	
	Savior from evil	links higher with lower	
	nature	Cosmic creation	
	beauty	Principle through which Father and Mother aspects of God express divine love.	
	gentleness		
	tenderness		
	kindness		
	infinite feeling		

Mirrors Family

Father	Father
Mother	Holy Spirit
Children	Son

Our help is in the name of the SOUL.

FEMININE PRINCIPLE: ME   Heart of flesh
　　　　　　　　　　　　Direct, sincere and honest
　　　　　　　　　　　　Compassion
　　　　　　　　　　　　Forgiveness
　　　　　　　　　　　　Love the weakness but not support it.
　　　　　　　　　　　　Non-judgment…evenness

GOD IN ALL APSECTS: THE GIFTS OF POSTERITY

I desire to know Thee God in all aspects: be it in the wounds, be it in the Resurrection. Unto this is grace fitting to be Who I AM. Amen. So be it. Alleluia.

Mother of even, Feminine Principle of God, I bow down before Thee to relish the blamelessness of my heritage. In causality, undiminished by light and/or darkness, sublime, divine in all aspects I behold my Maker, Creator of the divine Embrace. Be it unto ME, the gifts of posterity laid at my feet to behold my Maker in praise, in comfort, in sorrow, in grief, in joy, in all things forever. Amen. Thanks be to God.

THY/MY WILL

The light of my Soul responds to grace. Hail Mary, Queen of us all, reign down Your saving Love, to envelop us all as Your innocent children. We partake of the Bread of Life through Your commitment to Mankind: the hope to which we are called. Unblemished by stains of error and disgrace, we behold Thee as stronghold of the fort of All Justice, unwavering in love and mercy. Our openness to respond to this gift, Thy/My will be done: the only ingredient of worthy cause frees us to be at last home in the heart and soul.

THE VICTORY

This dawn of newness beckons me to respond and share with my fellowman this saving grace of posterity. Obliterated at last are torments of unknown proportions and accounts. We have won the victory through faith and perseverance. Trust, a new way of seeing, being, believing beyond the scope of the human lifts us to the divine embrace. The beckoning call awaits eagerly each soul's response. The joy-filled gladness of "Peace on Earth good will toward men." The ailing heart at last succumbs to the divine in gratefulness, thanks, purity of newness.

No more bleak skies for the heart that sees, the soul that hears. A new day is born for kindred spirits, joined hand in hand in merciful love: Heart, Spirit and Soul united in peaceful bliss, harmonious yet distinct, superb splendor, the envy of angels, no longer immersed in the clouds of glory. Man, beast, angels…distinct, yet separate, joined in the Reign of the Kingdom forever and ever. Amen.

THE GIFT OF POSTERITY: NEW LIFE

I seek to respond to the gifts and fruit of the Christ within.

I, so lost and fearful. I, so great and unworthy.

I, the treasured Lost Black Sheep in the fold.

Painful though it was, a journey of darkness:

The light broke through and granted freedom to the Soul.

How poorly understood today, I have a sad heart.

Because I want to help others understand the Gifts of the Kingdom:

Freedom of the Soul.

We, now as individuals, as priests, as communities, as states and nations live in the darkness. Let us wake up and respond to Life: life of a new generation, born to be new in the Soul. In reverence and awe, let us claim a new day, a new dawn to respond to the gift of posterity, New Life.

The theme of God's Justice is forgiveness. We just have to accept it and extend it to others. This will change the world in which we live.

MODIFY PERCEPTIONS

I seek to incorporate that Male aspect of Self to modify perceptions of Life. Be it unto me ever so boldly graced. I AM ME. This manifestation of realization is a process in the making. I ask my Savior and Lord Jesus Christ to walk by myself and embrace this Newness of Becoming. Thank You God. Alleluia.

THE LAW OF LOVE

What is the Law of Love? The Law of Love denotes that innocence achieved by man when he lets go of posterity: when he lets go of all. BE. Be open to receive the wisdom and proof of God in any moment encounter. Greed, desire are fruitless in this transcended state. The balance of opposites comes into play to make manifest the divine celebration of Life!

Thank You God for teaching and informing me of Your Way. I pray that I be open: let go of egocentric attitude, be an open vessel, receive the abundance of thy Creator-Redeemer-Lord of all the Universe. Amen. So be it. Alleluia. Thank You God for the sublime in all, through all, with all. Amen.

I pray this moment that I behave anew; that I accept healing grace Lord. I go before the holocaust and render it fruitful of good service and peace. Amen.

I ALLOW GOD TO BE GOD

Thank You God for your abundant grace, living and breathing in Your Love and light. I seek to mind my ways to be forever in Your grace and love.

I behold a new day dawning. My light shineth forth like the tulip in spring. The glistening of raindrops, the amber glow of dewdrops, the light shines forth to create a new day. I behold Thy Majesty before all, in all through all, with all Amen. I allow God to be God! Impose not my will on Thee, but respond to the abundance and free flow of Life.

THE SON OF GOD IS ME

You owe me a seal.

You owe a seal to the Son of God.

You owe a seal to the Son of man

Thank You God for Your bounty this day and all days.

You are infinity made whole.

You hold a secret of ME.

You hold a Son of ME.

You hold a saint of ME.

The Son of God is ME.

PROCESS: THE JOURNEY OF PITFALLS

I do the handiwork as a return to Thee, unencumbered. I love the silver and gold. I love the Soul.

Mary is the Yes to the sorrow. Mary is in lead of the Spirit. The Soul needs to be healed to be able to forgive. The spirit leads recognition.

"You hold the key of me. You are in lead of me."

Now my spirit needs to know me. Now, my spirit leads to know me. The Soul has informed the Spirit of the sorrow of the Soul. The Soul is even. This point reached, the Spirit is ready/able to respond to the Soul. The Spirit leads the recognition.

I deliver. I AM the hole in the heart. my Soul speaks to my Spirit… Mangled blood – mangled tissue. You are the obscene in ME. I now no longer want to hear/fear the Word of the Lord. I speak and live a new way.

The Lord of lies festered in grief is displaced by the Word.

> In the beginning was the Word
>
> And the Word was with God
>
> And the Word was God. Amen. – John 1:1

I belong to a new regime beholden to a deity of worth: the worth of my own Soul and Being propelled by grace, the grace to be ME. I encumbered am now unencumbered, free to be at last home in the Soul. I seek no revenge, but due process of law, Divine, to lift me from the depths of the shadows and raise me up to the heights of posterity. I, not in greed, but in justice to Man, to ME woman, feminine embodiment of Being. I belong. I AM ME blessed and thankful to be who I AM:

the journey of pitfalls without blame or malice. It has had to be, to be who and what I AM. Amen. So be it. Alleluia.

It is the virtue of the forgiven that creates the divine. I pray for the increase of the love of Christ within, so that I may be worthy of my calling, my mission. Amen. So be it. Alleluia.

TRUTH IS HORROR TO THE BLIND SOUL

The theme of forgiveness is perplexing to the Soul. The Soul in its essence knows truth. This truth has been concealed – veiled. The uncovering – unveiling is a life-long experience. Impatience does not rest well with this endeavor. The journey requires a persistence, faith, desire, passion, attention, with honest pure intention of the heart to seek, to know and to understand.

The advanced soul is led by Eros, spirit transformed in the light. Truth is horror to the blind soul. It creates what H. Emilie Cady calls "chemicalization." Modern expression is "spiritual emergence." This essentially means the new cannot be integrated, and therefore creates a state of chaos for the person. This can be a very painstaking experience. I suspect that some of our violence and suicide are a result of this emergence of the soul veiled with too much darkness to handle the incoming light. There is a dire need in this time of emerging light for communities to respond to this need of individuals going through these experiences. H. Emilie Cady, <u>Lessons in Truth</u> (Kansas City: Unity School of Christianity, 1941), 63-65.

TUG O WAR

My pencils are dulled. I need to sharpen them. It seems I've been too long removed from integral innate involvement: namely, in my Being. I have to eradicate the old; let go. It isn't as easy as it seems. I want to plant flowers, a garden. But my Soul wants redemption – other things beyond what one can see. I envision wholeness, wholeness of/in Being. This is my deep desire, wish. I get pulled/pushed many ways. Tug O War. Choices. My body, my limitations have to be engrossed in the moment: moment of Being. This is new to me. I have to learn as the child learns his/her numbers; how to read, etc. I need to be the child immersed in the moment of Being.

Unless the Lord build the house, they labor in vain who build it. Build a well supply. Tap into the deep reservoirs of nature. Take time to reflect and be. Be one with ME.

I will go in unto the altar of God. To God the Joy of ME.

Bless my spirits. Bless my Soul. Bless all of me. Amen. Alleluia. It seems so simple. but yet old engrained patterns aren't easy to eradicate. Be. Silence. Live fully. I'm used to noise, even though I don't like it. I'm used to business, even though I don't like it.

You are the Mother of Error transformed in the Love and Light.

THE LAW OF PURIFICATION

To purify my Being, I need to respond to the call of my Maker.

> Purify me, Oh Lord in all my elements.
> Make me an instrument fitting to behold Thee
> In glory and reverence; in awe and mortification.

The new wine seeps out of the vessel not yet strong enough in self-esteem (worth). I block the passage of Thee beholden to a deity. May my reverence bring me back to Eden to respond to the Kingdom of a new Order: Order of the Divine Light and Wisdom showered upon us through the Glory of the Resurrection, Resurrection of Eros.

The spirit world is new to my Being. The spirit world remains quiet when it is not manipulated or threatened.

Does the end justify the means?

Does the means justify the end? NO PROCESS.

Have we not all suffered enough? Let us put on the mind of Christ and abandon ourselves to the flow and spontaneity of grace: the grace heretofore claimed by the elite. Grace is registered to ALL, each and every person in his/her own way. The divine spark ignites a flame no longer to be extinguished: a flame of perpetual LOVE

> Freed of guilt and fear
>
> Freed of lack of belief
>
> Freed from inequality

By the love and forgiveness pervading all Being.

Let us not worry about ends and means, means and ends. Love does not judge. LOVE hinders not the transformation of mind. The HEART, the true embellished in splendor, judgment released, the TRUTH abounds in LOVE.

My heart speaks out in awe and wonder: creation manifested through the Divine Embrace. Be it unto me unforgiven, now forgiven for all posterity to see THE DIVINE AT WORK: ENDLESS.

My Soul responds justified by Being. A new dawn breaks forth to shelter the poor in spirit. We are One in all, through all, with all as the Christ principle operates, fully, effectively with grace operative in each given moment of Being.

I behold Thee, my Maker blasphemed by no one; borne of fruit of the spirit.

> Bless my Spirit
> Bless my soul
> Blest be the Holocaust

No longer shrouded in mystery, but exposed to the light of Grace: dawn of newness encompassing all earth, all being, All Oneness. the handiwork of God forgiving and forgiven. Amen. Thanks be to God.

May the Soul of Justice reign down upon us on Earth to proclaim a new day of painstaking glory manifested through the Holy Spirit now and forever. Amen. Alleluia. Alleluia. Alleluia.

HUMILITY

I stand. I kneel. I prostrate myself before my God and Maker. Helpless though I am, I giveth power through grace to act out the divine calling manifested in Love: Love of neighbor, Love of self, Love of all that is, God's creation. I humbled through grace, grace bestowed so bounteously to me, a child of God, to each, to all of us. We are all One in the divine Sonship: blessed, forgiven and forgiving. let us live in the peace and harmony promised us in the divine fellowship of the entire universe.

Holy   Holy   Holy

Blessed art Thou our God with thankful hearts abiding in grace

Forever and ever. Amen. Alleluia.

Be it unto Me the gift of blessedness. I behold my Maker each day, each moment in awe and wonder, the power of the universe squelched by the divine calling in each Soul to respond to the gift of Posterity – NEW LIFE.

The wound of Sacredness lifts us out of torment, torment of Soul and Spirit; the heart pierced, the sorrow of the Soul released to the Joy of perfection in the divine Sonship, embraced, embracing all that is. Amen. Alleluia.

Sorrow released, the vessel is ready to be filled: each Soul gifted to respond to the unique calling, that manifestation of God (principle) made present in our life-lives. The gift of Christ, the new born sheltered, protected, made ready to leave its mark on posterity.

This Joy embraced beholden to a deity – Son of God, we make the Way: the Way affordable to all, blameless in the sight of the Lord Our God.

Our participation in Divine Creation takes hold. We participate in mutual love. Our God awaits and beckons each soul to respond to the call, the call of this Divine Embrace.

May the Joy of Saint Francis and all the saints support us in our endeavors to respond to the call of Joy of Resurrection.

WHAT ARE THE FRUITS OF THE JOY OF RESURRECTION?

Blameless in Posterity	Faithfulness
Forthrightness	Knowledge
Blessedness	Temperance
Albeit Son of God	Godliness
Virtuousness	Brotherly Kindness
Dependability	Charity (Love)

HOW DO WE/I RESPOND TO THE CALLING IN GRACE OF OUR BROTHERS AND SISTERS WHO FALL BY THE WAYSIDE: THE SOUL ENCRUSTED WITH GRIEF, FEAR, EMBELLISHED IN SELF-HATE AND DESTRUCTION, PURSUANT OF MEANS AND ENDS BEYOND OUR ABILITY TO RESPOND OR COPE?

I bow my head and prostrate myself before You Lord Jesus to come to our/my aid. In grief-stricken array, we are at a loss to respond: to respond to the needs of the violent rejection of Self.

Be it unto me/Me ever so graced to call upon Your aid in healing love to the afflicted Soul, the Soul created and loved by You Who gave Your only Son Jesus Christ to be Savior for all mankind through Your most glorious death, resurrection and ascension into heaven to respond to the needs of all man/womankind.

I ask Your favor and blessing to respond to the particular need of NAME a message of deliverance to the love, light and wisdom of Mother/Father God. Amen.

I ask Your favor and blessing on all those involved in helping charitable Christ action to pour out Your love and wisdom to instruct in ways to respond to NAME'S need in the name of the Christ Who honors and cares for us all. Amen. So be it. Alleluia.

Grant us discernment, wisdom and love of the Christ to respond in each particular moment to the need at hand. Amen.

May the Soul of NAME be lifted to the glories of heaven and be given peace.

THE SACRIFICE OF MOTHERHOOD

Be it unto me fittingly graced with the gifts of posterity.

BLESSED BE MY SOUL encumbered in sin and grief.

BLESSED BE MY BEING in fortuitous grace and blessedness.

BLESSED BE ME, the gift of the divine embrace.

BLESSED BE ALL HUMANITY in error, in truth, in wickedness, in sloth, in greed, in endless torment.

BLESSED BE ALL CREATION, all that is in God's glory and mercy.

BLESSED BE WE SOULS WHO REPENT AND FORGIVE: in repenting and forgiving, the divine light and love of the Christ is expressed through us, with us and in us.

BLESSED BE WE CO-CREATORS: in virtuous being and living we express the divine embodiment of Being.

BLESSED BE WE SONS AND DAUGHTERS OF GOD – EROS: Spirit resurrected unto the glorious manifestation of all that is and will be now and forever. Amen.

BLESSED BE MY SOUL ENCUMBERED, NOW UNENCUMBERED through Mary's YES to the Glory of Resurrection (Resurrection of Eros).

May our Souls be lifted up to the glories of heaven and fill the earth with PEACE ON EARTH, good will toward man and woman. Amen. So be it. Alleluia.

ON BEING HUMAN

I in bare feet walk
The path of no return
Embellished with gifts of creative force
I in bare feet walk.

To tread the ground in toil and labor
I in bare feet walk
Superfluous are the many throes of life's woes
I in bare feet walk.

In humble awakenings
I come to know
Bit by bit, woe by woe
I in bare feet walk

The dirt, the mud, the grass, the mire
The stream the flow
The flow of grace
Embracing all that is.

I in bare feet walk
Embodiment of being take hold
Being who and what I AM
I in bare feet walk.

MODERN SOJOURNERS' CHALLENGE

Eight Stages of the Spiritual Journey

Full humanness comes about through effort and calm. Barbarian manners and actions are not characteristic of the truly human. Let us not fool ourselves. The true human embodiment of man means:

1. Initiation of the struggle to be who You/We are.

This stage encompasses development and moderation in all sense appetites, be it drug, sex, food, money, consumerism, idolization, etc. Basic to this stage of development is living by the Law of Moses – the Ten Commandments. In the tradition of the East-Buddhism, this is the eight-fold path. The emotions can run rampant. This stage may take a lifetime, maybe more. The desire and passion within the person is a key factor in this development. Grace is always present. All that is required is openness of the heart to receive.

2. This stage of development can be called the Movement of the Soul.

It is the deep inner stage that cannot be well described because it is in the darkness and hidden. It can be characterized by an element of chaos in the struggle to birth the true Self-YOU-ME. This stage requires withdrawal, observation, reflection, introspection. The world is viewed differently than before. Desires of things past fall by the wayside. Sorrow and grief are major components of this stage. It is emptying – letting go – acceptance of all that is. It is the stage of repentance and forgiveness.

3. This stage may be characterized as revelation or epiphany.

It is a deepening in conscious awareness that penetrates the soul. The person in this sojourn knows the meaning of prayer on a new level. It is no longer rote-ritual. It is a creative force propelled by grace. This is a stage of vulnerability, full realization of sojourners' helplessness in the sight of God. It is the opening of LOVE: the crack in the door. It is the stage of will and desire of Thy/My will be done.

4. This stage of development is characterized by the awakening heart.

It is truly the onset of full humanness in expression. It is the gradual unfoldment of true compassion, humility and mutual love. It is the stage where Eros has come home to the Soul and leads. This resurrection of Eros, a divine embrace transforming evil, initiates the birth of the true Self. Without this union of the Soul with Eros, man cannot be fully human. It is this process that is needed and will transform the world. It is an acknowledgment and understanding of our holiness: the essential awe and wonder we live in each moment.

5. This is not a stage of a sigh of relief – I've made it. The inner struggle-war continues between the soul and spirit.

Emotions seek to devour. One must stand back, distance oneself and be the observer. Also, it is a time plagued by discouragement. One can't be in control of all the baggage. The total dependence on God is acknowledged. It is a time when persistence, fortitude are essential to the ongoing process. The Soul requires constancy in prayer. It is a time of developing greater humility to love the Soul but not support weaknesses. It is a period of increased passion to be One with the Father: Thy/My will be done. It is a learning in Being – Puer Childlike Simplicity. It is a beholding in Me – Thee. It is an emptying to make way for the true Self, Son of God, formed and molded clay grounded in my nature. The waters of unknown depths are stilled.

6. This stage is the point of quickening the spirit to respond to the desire of the heart.

The process is ongoing. Temptations erupt to be apart from Thee. The feminine principle of God is experienced: Mother of Even. Dualities fall by the wayside. The mystery of Life is revealed. One is no longer innocent/ignorant. It is a call of our mentor, The Christ: to be One with our Maker. Like a lion prey I emerge in the nakedness of the Self.

7. This is a period of a deepening of faith and trust.

It is a period of letting go of illusions to become the servant of God to fulfill service and purpose. The Dabar (creative) and Eros (passion) harmoniously bring Love (content) and Justice (form) into rightful measure into Being. There is still a need for purification of the Heart. This process is unknown and hidden to the Wayfarer. The mystery of Self continues to unfold. Mary, Queen of Life delivers the message of Will-Being in response to our call.

8. This is a period of renewal of commitment to respond to the grace of no boundaries.

Trust brings the change: change of heart purified, sublime. This freedom allows/propels the soul to continually respond to NEW LIFE. It is a time to erase SLOTH through the power of the Holy Spirit. Masking the Shadow of Even is dropped. United in Thy/My Being; in Thy/My Heart, we commune in solitude to strengthen and uplift the Self and World. We full knowingly respond to Truth, the truth of helplessness. Eros, transformed in the light and love is the blessing of GRACE.

It is the full acknowledgment of the responsibility of sojourners to respond to Truth: come home to the heart; elevate and restore the human-divine relationship through the Law of Faith.

To be continued in the next work of mercy: God's Gift to Humanity.

PART SEVEN
The next work of mercy.

GOD,
GIFT TO HUMANITY

THE NEXT WORK OF MERCY

What a moment of exultation I have in communing with the Lord Jesus Christ, whither He guides me and leads me. I, in exultation, commend Thee/Me to behold my Maker: unaccountable – accountable in pilfering, in exile, in grief. Behold ME/Thee in all, through all, with all. I blasphemed by no One/one am embellished through Faith: Faith in our Fathers and heritage to come to grips with the stipends of grief.

In exaltation, I commend Thee to the Spirit, the Spirit of everlasting Life – Life in the church and world. You are My beloved servant anchored in the Gospel truth of redemption and everlasting Life. May You/I be fitting vessels to uphold the wealth of posterity decreed upon us by the innermost sanctum of decrees from our Lord Jesus Christ Himself, Redeemer and Blessed forevermore. Amen.

I ask my Lord and Savior to instruct me well regarding current undertakings in the world: tarot, astrology, numerology, communion with the dead, psychic readings. Of what help or distractions are these for Your people? If we are in process of unfoldment in upholding the faith in our Lord Jesus Christ, can I be led and protected through Faith regardless of snares of the devil: that existence which propels man to be what he is not?

My Lord, I come to You no longer in grief but in Joy of Resurrection, Resurrection of the Spirit to behold Thee in all, through all, with all in the name of Jesus Christ, our Lord. Amen.

No, it is not harmful to be who and what you are in any setting. you are My child, protected, safeguarded from any and all snares of evil. Amen. So be it. Alleluia. Thanks be to God.

My Lord, I pray to You for humility to be constantly Your servant. Let me not lapse or grow tepid in my love or faith for, with and in You. Thank You Father/Mother God. So be it. Amen.

I behold my Maker in awe and grief to be redeemed by no One, through One, with One. All is well in the gifts of posterity, New Life. Jesus the Christ, Savior, Redeemed, Blessed, may I respond to this call in grace, grace with no boundaries to be lifted up to posterity, posterity of Being, Being One with Thee. Amen. No one can destroy me but myself. I have the risen Christ to respond to my Savior in all times, all places, all things. Forever Protector, Mentor, Disciple.

It is a helpless state to respond to, to be a vessel for the risen Christ. This is my mission, my work: to be an instrument of Redemption beholden to my God, my Maker.

May the Spirit of the Risen Christ beseech Thee to make me a fitting instrument to respond to the call of Grace and Purity of Heart. Amen. I you most humble servant accept the gift of posterity – NEW LIFE. This is a free gift. I thank You God with all my heart, soul, strength, mind in this order NOW! So be it. Alleluia. You are me in expression. Thank You God.

My tears, my grief can never express the gratitude I feel, believe, do. Amen. I in seeking truth had been tormented in fear, in grief, in abandonment, in deceit, in calamitous events. you Lord never let me down. In persistence and fortitude I persevered. You did and do respond. I like Thomas have had to be shown. Thank You, my God, my Savior, my Redeemer. I know I have tread where angels fear to tread. Thank You, God.

Strip me of egocentric consciousness. I must be Your servant. The world has too much darkness. may I be a fitting example to show a glimmer of light and the way. There is far too much suffering; it is not human. Let us respond to Your call and accept Your invitation to the wedding. Let us be prepared. Show us the way. Amen. Thank You God. Alleluia. Amen.

We receive Truth when we are ready to embrace it.

I AM the delight of the SOUL. I live and breathe ONE ME.

I AM that I AM who I AM what I AM. I AM. I AM ME. Alleluia. Amen.

It is fitting to behold Me, the object of creation, the whole Being emphasized in the gospel message. unjustified, justified: the paradox of all creation. We are fitting to behold our Maker. The Father and I are One.

Into the Godhead, I pierce the beam of light and radiate into nothingness; dispelled by the fear of disgrace, I move on to new horizons oblivious to my Being. It is a welcome path, a welcome search into the unknown abyss, Co-creator with God. May I be a fitting vessel to proceed on mark. Trappings dropped by the wayside to behold my Maker, through One, with One, in One. One in all.

To fathom this belief, this discovery is a momentous task. I penetrate the mystery of the divine embrace, with One, in One, through One. It is a welcome search, search home to the heart. The Heart of unexplored depths. May we fathom the depths of unknown propelled by grace in trust and faith. Amen. So be it. Alleluia.

The journey is filled with surprises unbeknown to the Wayfarer. The mystery of ordeal continues. It is not for the faint in heart. Unexplored depths emerge in succession. I am at that point of perplexed mystery waiting to birth the unknown into creation: creation with, in and through God. Amen. So be it. Alleluia. Thank You God.

COMMUNION OF SOUL AND SPIRIT

Soul

    Oh! Be it unto me that is reprehensible (blameworthy).

    I come to You in blindness.

    But in faith and trust You lead me.

    I still in weakness persist.

Spirit

    Halt! Bear forth good news.

    Thou shalt be established in the firmament.

    Not blind faith, but faith-knowing Thy God.

    All is well.

Soul

    I tempted in weakness

    Must circumvent

    Claim the GOOD-NEW

    Salvation and forgiveness of humanity.

Spirit

    Yes. It is fitting to behold Thee

    Enamored in grace.

    Pittance for the shallow illusions.

    Be established in grace. Recompense.

Soul

    Be it unto Me/Thee

    Thy favor granted.

    Blessed is the Kingdom

    Now and forever.

We so unworthy to behold Thee fall down trodden by illusion again and again and again. Let us be propelled by grace through trust and faith to be what we are meant to be: God in expression. God in action. Through the divine embrace of the Silence to behold Thee/Me. Amen. Thanks be to God. Alleluia.

SONG OF THE SOUL

Oh Blessed is My Soul
The Joy in the Morning Sun
May My light shine through
Thee to Me.

Blessed is My Being
Extended to Me through Thee
My light is
Amen.

Out of the depths
I arise in Glory
To shine the light of Thee
In Me.

THE PROPHET

Who and what is the prophet: the prophetic voice that keeps us protected, always steering us onward in the right direction to counter illusion? May we be open to receive and listen to the prophet of God-Divine Wisdom-Justice-Love continually. I beckon me/you to come to fresh spring waters to drink daily, lest we forget who we are and why we are here. Saint Augustine says, "Love and do what you like." This seems to imply that inner bode of Being: being at one with all, through all, in all. This is not achieved automatically. Openness to grace beckons us to respond to the message of good will. Peace on earth.

May I be fit to endure the struggles and temptations counter to the goal of Redemption. Amen. I have struggles today and yesterday. I feel like chattel in relation to the patriarchal control and influence of society. May the good Lord teach and show me how foolish my/our illusions are. Through the working of the Holy Spirit, I pray for protection and uplifting of the self to be Who I AM. Amen. Thanks be to God. Alleluia.

I speak not of mission or purpose, but of divine right: divine right of my Being, beholden to no one. May the grace forthcoming help me to respond to my mentor, the Christ. I AM ME. It is fitting to behold ME. I flounder and grapple at times. I forget who I AM. I need and take this moment of solace to establish more clearly and deeply the path of no return. I Your humble servant speak up. What is it to me? Grace forthcoming in the mud and mire? I, expectant seek greater things beholden to a deity. May I continue to behold Thee in awe and wonder.

The perilous journey continues. Emotions trample on blessings. Forgiveness, the divine work of mercy is forthcoming when I open the heart to receive Thee. OBEDIENCE! Thy/My will be done. Amen. (Command lower self-unconscious to respond to Higher Self). The soul can respond in error. But it is the result, the consequences that teach us. We need to pay attention.

I behold Thee/Me in all, through all, with all. Blessed is my Soul To be One with Thee. Amen. Thank You God. Alleluia.

We are each drawn individually to share in the expression of God's Love. This timing seems to be a mutual harmonious movement on the part of the Wayfarer and God. Oh be it unto my soul to respond rightly to the glories of the Resurrection. Alleluia. Amen. So be it. Thanks be to God.

My light shines forth like the morning dove.

LOVE

"Love is not love

Which alters when it alteration finds,

Or bends with the remover to remove:"

William Shakespeare Sonnet 116

Love

The impediment of evil

Displaces all reason

In the context of man's being.

Love is contrary to modern thought

Love glimpses of the primate veiling

Love is heretofore unseen in its fullest dimension

Love is yet to be discerned and discovered.

Love's way is a mystery
Unfolding in the universe
Love embellishes all that is
In non-judgment, it stands before God.

Love holds us bound to no limit.
Love is the guiding light that leads
Out of darkness and chaos
Creation continues.

Let our prayer be overshadowed with divine grace
To behold our Maker
Sublime, Pure, Holy
Devoid of hostility.

It is fitting to behold Thee/Me/You
In awe and wonder and sacred reverence
We continue in our struggle
In our search for Truth. Amen.

THE HIGHER DICTATES OF THE SOUL

I Your humble servant respond to grace. I accept my position of wealth: wealth of being – all in all, one in all, all in one.

What are the higher dictates of the Soul? Exclusiveness is ruled out. We are one among many, many among One, in One. I – Our forefathers granted us favor to behold Thee in awe and wonder and austere judgment. In order to become that universal Man, we respond in a new way to grace, wealth of being, all in all, One in all, all in One.

What is my calling this day? I am bent to receive; I am ambivalent in many ways. The throes of life perplex me in the gridiron of defeat. I rise to the Master: to the call, the call of grace stifled by no one. It can be heard in any setting. Dumbfound though I be, I become a new man/woman in spite of me. It is my/our calling. The universal wealth and riches are ever present to our beckon call. It is time to respond this moment to be renewed in faith and trust. The scattered seeds in raging winds come to a halt: focused, dynamic union of being, being One with Thee.

> Ask! Help us Oh Lord in our need.
>
> Receive! Splendor in grace, answers to every detail.
>
> We respond in harmony, peace and dominion over the Earth.
>
> God! Gift to Humanity.

I, scattered ask the good Lord to focus my attention: attention to the details of existential life. I have difficulty with clutter. I get caught up in details. I'm so fussy even when it comes to dealing with junk. If my weakness be my strength, let me direct it to the Almighty God Redeemer. Even the junk seems holy and alive. I in reverence and awe seem to be bombarded. My spirit is so creative, I can manifest the most wonderful and godly out of junk. Lord, please help me to focus on You and forget about the junk. I feel that I have a weakness here that needs circumventing. May I through all this display the fruitage of the vine. In elaborate testimony I reveal myself to Thee. I want to be rid of wastefulness, and take on the focused discipline of ruliness, order, obsessions dropped. Help me in my need. Amen. Thanks be to God. Alleluia.

I'm interested in so many things. They are all of You and holy. Help me to focus on my greater need to be Thee/Me in expression. Amen. I feel like I'm getting rid of baggage so I can be the fuller expression of Thee. I get tired of doing routine and mundane. Perhaps this is good discipline for my Soul. I need to be prepared to advance the tenets of the Path Thou has given and spelled out for Me. Amen. Thanks be to God. Alleluia. Alleluia. Alleluia.

Praise is always fitting for my Redeemer, Savior of mankind. Thanks be to God. God's Justice is always expressed in and through the act of forgiveness: forgiveness of self, others and acceptance of forgiveness from God. Our help is in the light of the Soul.

> Out of the depths I cry to Thee Oh Lord.
>
> Have mercy on me and the brethren.

Oh be it unto me fitting in grace to behold Thee, Redeemer of humanity.

> I ask for help regarding _____.

Pray for _____. Love _____. Be present for _____. Believe in _____.

We need to be sensitive to spirit communication. Spirit wants to show us how to respond. Meditate. I let go of visual and feel the Beingness.

THE HARVEST OF NO RETURN

I need a more cerebral life now. It is difficult to be occupied with the mundane. My Soul does not like it. I need to be more flexible, let go as much as I can of mundane, focus on Thee, the object of my desire. Exhilarated into oblivion, I bestow the merits of wonder and awe. It is grace fitting for a deity. In splendor, in ardor, in magnificence I come forth to reap the harvest of no return. I AM ME. I cannot return to old ways. I am like the cocoon larvae turning into the butterfly. This birthing means a new road. A new way.

DEVOTION TO THE CELEBRATION OF LIFE

Dear Lord, I ask Your favor and blessing to respond to the call, the grace, the path of o return to move forward in this venture to be, become who I AM meant to be. it is fitting. It is just. Solitude is a must for me. Space, Nature, Stay grounded, Study, Love Relationships, Balance family; take care of physical needs to I can respond gladly, gleefully to the awakened call of Grace – this path of leadership devoted to the celebration of Life. I AM Thine Own Power Bestowed meant to be brought to fruition through the Holy Spirit upon me. Thanks be to God. Amen. Alleluia. I need to be attentive to this call. it is my destiny to Be and respond to the invitation to love. This is my wish. This is my desire – to see the world transformed in love and light. I respond in trust, in faith, in hope, in love. I give my all to this divine commitment and grace. Destiny shall not be thwarted. So be it. Alleluia. Thank You God. May You be worshipped forever and ever by All, by ME/me. Thanks be to God. Amen.

FACING THAT INNER ME

Oh be it unto me gloriously blessed to have been chosen in the drift of things to make amends; to find solace in facing that inner me: the enemy of all time, Satan if you will, and appease those hostile aspects of me. Thank You God for this blessing and deliverance from evil and torment. Amen.

ON SEXUALITY

Our universe is electrical, with opposite forces coming together to be One. This union of opposites is diametrically opposed to scattered randomness. It is an essentially orchestrated harmonious encounter that embraces all yet divides into that unique expression: animal mineral, vegetable, human being. Striving for balance is an ongoing process. The integration of the parts within the self is paramount for wholeness/wholesomeness. This means integrating anima-animus, mother, father, child, senex, shadow. This is not an easy task, but necessary in the evolution of man to be what he is meant to be: the full expression of divinity in our world.

> What a momentous calling.
> What a momentous gift.
> What a profound awakening.

To be what/who we are meant to be: fully human – fully divine. My message for the LGBTQIA+ is the same as for the heterosexual and eunuch. This integration of the aspects of the self help us to become who and what we are meant to be.

This raises the question of all identifiers. We must love our strengths and our weaknesses; however, we cannot support our weaknesses no matter how we identify ourselves…no matter how we expect others to see us. The road to integration of male/female is difficult and a great challenge for all.

I pray that we be further enlightened. Amen. Thanks be to God. Alleluia.

> Praise to You Lord, Maker of the Universe.
> Praise to You always, in adversity, in comfort, in all ways and means.
> Praise forever and ever. Amen.

Thank You God for this day. Amen.

Blessed is my/our Soul forever and ever. Amen.

MOTHER OF EVEN: FEMININE PRINCIPLE OF GOD

What is the Mother of Even? This expression demystifies the mystical. It elaborates on our will-beingness. It embraces truth: truth of all, in all, through all. It brings us to that point of awareness: consciousness if you will, to respond to grace, the grace of forgiveness no matter what the stipends of grief. This is the opening of the door: the opening of the door to NEW LIFE.

Justification by Faith is explicitly adhered to: that is, believing and receiving with honest, pure intention of the heart. It incorporates the facet of non-judgment, a key to our will-being.

In the throes of complex explanations and arguments exist the gridiron of defeat. Defeated, we must not be! We must move on and forward in faith of ourselves, God and neighbor to bear the burden of defeat. We rise up time after time to dispel the Age-old pattern to allow for the NEW. Make way for the Glorious Resurrection of Man. The stage compelling us forward and onward is the feminine birthing of that divine innocence: sonship – divine child to rescue us through the torments of war with the self; expressed as fear, guilt, rage, anger, dualism, unforgiveness.

WOMAN: MOTHER OF HUMANITY

Be it unto me sacredly blessed; beholder of Truth-Wisdom of ages past.

I block no one from grace of Being.

The Wisdom of Ancient Books of Old throw light on the destiny of man. We are in the throes of whirlwind and chaos catapulted by the unforeseen event of the future. May we be blessed in every moment with the grace of the ancients to bear the fruit of our forefathers: sacrifice of will-being. I, enamored in grace circumvent the pitfalls of/for posterity. We, behold to a Deity of such grace and stature. We, beholden to the Son of God Son of Man: servant of Almighty Power of God. The unfolding scroll: the Seal of Love pounces like wolves on prey. God's Love so tantamount to alter the course of history in spite of me. Conscious will-beings: the magnitude of stupendous feats to behold the Master, Sublime, Divine, in the embrace of the Divine Child, Son of God.

THE WAY OF THE DESTROYER

The ambivalence of man is in his inability to focus on the mundane. The particular needs of the moment dictate the task at hand. We go off on tangents into the worlds of unknown without a clue to our own basic need to be centered in our God-given path. This brings us to a halt. The Destroyer enters to destruct old ways. Chaos and question ensues. The depth of unknown mystery are plummeted to find and discover Me. The balance of opposites come into play. Masculine-Feminine poles intermix and play games, hide and seek with us. The shadow emerges and projects its destructive tentacles to destroy the good, the desirable. After much pain and suffering, the defeated self emerges, emptied to begin anew. The trial and error path reveals to man by the fruit it bears. Generation after generation may be stilted in a destructive mode. The conscious awakening motive is finally drawn upon to turn things around. This process of climbing laboriously up the mountain path to victory is finally established.

It is time to bring this process into focus and participation by the masses: God's people. Our institutions now call and cry out for drastic change: a tearing down of the old to build the NEW JERUSALEM. The physical temple (body as well as built structures) is a mirror which precedes man's destined path to tear down the old to build the NEW. This process takes place within each individual life and is carried out to destroy and create the new institutional structures that reflect the Kingdom of God. The within and without are brought harmoniously in balance. This is the Vision, the moment of Man in an ordered universe to bring order out of chaos.

Dear God,

How can I change getting caught up in other people's drama (wants, needs, distractions) so I can become more ME?

The CALL......................lack of resources, harmony, support or order in my life.

The RESPONSE ....take responsibility for my state of life.

                              Seek healing of wounds or areas of powerlessness
reflecting scarcity in outer life.

                              The saddest resource to waste is a human life.

PROCLAMATION ....YOU are the Mother of EVEN!
                              YOU are the deliverer of the Soul of ME!

POSTSCRIPT

I have written this during <u>Tosca</u> (Radio National Broadcast). It is amazing to me how the operas depict the tragedy of our own life-lives if we do not proceed with the birthing process. It is time to change the story of Opera to include the Glory of Resurrection to create models of birthing and NEW LIFE following death. Opera depicts the archetypes.

We can respond to archetypes who promote LIFE. It is my hope that we have a Renaissance of Opera with LIFE after death as the motivating force for Man-Woman-Child-Mankind. With Mary's help, we will find the way and bravely respond. Thank you Mary, Mother of God.

My Soul is so weary, it grieves. It is through Your YES that we find not only Hope but realization of the Kingdom – NEW LIFE. I am grieving. I am saying goodbye to the soul of old. I am responding to NEW LIFE. It is my wish. It is Your wish. Amen. Thank You Mary. You are my guide. You are my armor and strength. Thank You. Blessed be God forever. Amen.

The drama of the Soul is ended. Now is the time to renew the Earth. You are my guide, Mother of God: MARY. I have only my own experience, the Divine Light within to guide me. Thank You God. I AM Your beloved servant. Let each of us share our gift/gifts to the fullest to benefit everyone's journey. Amen. Thank You God. Amen. Alleluia.

We have loved the Soul. We have loved the sorrow. Goodbye forever. I/We move on to new horizons. <u>Tosca</u> has helped me. Thank You God. *The Sound of Music* also speaks of letting go. Birth anew!

I now embrace the NEW, the unknown. May my path be filled with the flower petals of old in ritual procession as a child dropping flower petals in the aisles in church. I have fond memories, now more meaningful since our children have never had this ritual experience.

It is my hope and love that God will provide the gift of LOVE to ALL. Amen. So be it. Alleluia. Thanks be to God.

Death of the soul is required to experience NEW LIFE: Resurrection of the Spirit.

My work now is to experience the process of change:

>Death of the SOUL. Birth of the SPIRIT.

TRANSFORMATION

I let the night creep upon Me

I let the shadows descend on my heart

I let the Earth become polluted

With the soul's garbage and defeat.

I now wake up to the sorrow

To change the scene of ugliness

Now I work in my soul, in my heart

To change the distorted to the real.

In perseverance I proceed

To change: to change the real

To transform the known to the unknown

To create a new model of Wealth of Being.

Transformation is radical

What is my role – play?

May I be open to respond to the call

Birth anew.

MARY, come to my/our aid! You are my/our model, guide, light. Amen. Alleluia. I/We need to express that NEW MODEL. MARY-GOD show us the way to be the living fountain of the Christ!

REFLECTIONS ON BEING HUMAN

I AM. I'm sad and disappointed. What has our value system evolved to? I sorrowfully grieve at the present state of affairs – worldwide: Kuwait, Rwanda, Viet Nam, the Holocaust, Oklahoma Bombing, to name a few events that encompass our historical experience. With Joseph Conrad through the character of Kurtz I expound, "The horror! The horror!" For those who wish to take time to reflect, I share my own views on being human. It is my hope that in conscious awakening, we can respond humanly.

There is an unwritten code in each of us. We are the embodiment of Being taking hold as a new species undergoing remarkable differentiation. As we proceed into the New Age, the Piscean stronghold will be loosed – let go. The Sorrows of the Soul will be released. The empty – emptied vessel will receive a new stage of awareness heretofore unknown. This will replace the old. A new dawn arises. The Holy Spirit fully activated by the centuries prophetic voice will herald in a new regime.

What is it likened to? A garden of paradise: truly the Garden of Eden for those present to behold the dawn of a new era. With the erasing of the slate so to speak, of the negative and positive poles, a new Man, the mind of Christ clothes us. We are Radiant Beings. Let us prepare for this event in our constancy, in our watchfulness, in our connectedness with God, with Earth, with our fellow brother and sister. We are no longer shrouded in the mystery of old. We live the mystery, fully activated in our being Who and What we are. The divine embrace takes hold and propels us in a new way. May we be enlightened further in these endeavors and events in history. Thanks be to God. Alleluia.

The fourth aspect to make us whole in the Trinitarian drama: that is, the Feminine Principle of God takes hold to complete the Quadrant. This activation allows the release of the negative-positive (dualistic) waves to propel us into this new mode of Being – WHOLESOME BEING.

THE WORKS OF FAITH

When we enter the Sage of Son of God, God the Father births the Son of ME. In this sense, we become true Co-creators with God. This mutuality/interchange is paramount now in our time of need.

As Co-creators, we align ourselves fully with the will of the Father: Thy/My will be done. This harmonious mutual interchange is liken to a dance perfectly executed between partners. On a grander scale, it is like a chorus and orchestra performing in perfect sync. This is the goal for man to come to: that point in development in which the harmony and peace are spontaneous at any given moment. Can we imagine a world, a universe so beautifully awesome?

Let us begin now with the Works of Faith. Amen. Thanks be to God. Alleluia.

OH LIFE, OH BEAUTEOUS LIFE!
FOREVER NEW – PASSION OF THE GOD/GODDESS

How can it be other than One among many. Many Gods/Goddesses we are.

Violetta Rigoletto your Soul dies that you may find LIFE
Your search is not futile
Come back, Oh Spirit: refresh your boughs
Respond to LIFE: the renewed Home of ages to come.

Posterity beckons Thy beauty forthcoming to live in the New Self
The Heart manifest in Eternal Mystery
The Self, perplexed and hidden no more; exposed to world view and acclaim

Be You/We blessed.

Violetta Rigoletto Eternal Beauty live on
The shadow faded
The bright light beaming to destroy no One
You live! Violetta Rigoletto FOREVER NEW!

HYPNOSIS AND THE TRANSCENDENT FUNCTION EXPLAINED AND CONTRASTED

The hypnotic state is not to be confused with the transcendent function. Hypnosis is that state or condition of the body in which lighter or deeper trance is induced. The subject is brought into quiet of mind and body. The outward forces of the universe control the subject, in that the subject is guided or steered in a certain direction concerning (more or less) specific timing and or events. The occurrence of past lives in historic time frames, the womb experience, the birthing process, events of early childhood or the like are brought into focus. Oftentimes, the subject experiences traumatic events that are real, for example, a violent death, a difficult birth, being another person in another lifetime.

The value of hypnosis in many circumstances is not to be ignored. Emotional blocks or inhibition can be released through this method. This releasing is essential to the growth and welfare of the person.

The transcendent function on the other hand, is the encounter of the divine embrace. It acknowledges the helplessness of man on his own, his sin in error and ignorance, his complete disrespect for what he truly is; is meant to be and in fact is, a child of God. As a result, this obstinacy, this distraction, this road to by-ways creating chaos and perdition translates into suffering evil.

The information given here is not new, but is repeatedly stated in a new way. The purest examples have been passed down to us by the Buddha and Jesus. Man has thwarted the path and not paid attention. As a result, the road back to the light and love of the Christ has become difficult for most of us. The simplest way to the right path is opening the heart to activate the grace of no limit or boundaries available to all, for all, in all.

May we be given up to the Body of Christ to lift us from the perdition and gloom and respond to the call of our Beloved in grace forevermore. Thanks be to God. Alleluia. Alleluia. Alleluia.

UNION OF OPPOSITES

From balancing the opposites, we move to union of opposites The Intelligent One.

> We are the body and blood of Christ.
>
> We are the pierced heart.
>
> WE are the wounded Soul
>
> We are the body, soul, spirit, heart united as One.
>
> We are the mind of Christ.
>
> We are the light of the World.

The union of the oppositions within us relieves us of anxiety and fear. We are the storm called at sea and calmed – stopped in the heart. (Emotions no longer rule us). The pierced heart gushes forth NEW LIFE, that is, compassion for all, with all, in all. This is the "demonstration of the realization of God," most ardently understood by followers of the <u>Infinite Way</u>, taught and demonstrated by Joel Goldsmith. It is also the criteria used by the Catholic Church to verify a miracle. We are beholders of Thee. Amen. Gratias.

May the New World Order be established in the firmament. Thanks be to God.

> Blessed be God
>
> Blessed be His Holy Name
>
> Blessed be me transformed
>
> Blessed be all that is and will be.
>
> Forever and ever. Amen.

Achieving balance and harmony between conscious and unconscious is an on-going process in individuation.

RESTORATION OF TRUE RELATIONSHIP

I AM myself and ME totally obliterated by the sea of divine light means coming into fruiting in the union of the opposites, that is, oppositions within the self. This truly is the goal of mankind, the reestablishment of long forgotten past: the restoration of true relationship, human – divine/human.

This stage arrived, the full development of the unique personality within the divine can be expressed: that unique co-creative aspect of God that cannot be copied. A most fitting analogy is the patchwork quilt (each piece different and unique). If one piece is missing, the quilt cannot be fully complete. This shows us the unique importance of each and every Soul in God's creation. It also shows the importance of the integration and balance of all aspects within the total person.

May we respond to the call and duty to fulfill our mission, our inbuilt code to bring about harmony in all, through all, with all in the name of Jesus Christ. Amen. Thanks be to God. Alleluia.

THE DIVINE ESSENCE OF PURITY IS ONE WITH THEE

I behold Thee/Me in all aspects. The wonders of humanity are manifest in, through and with the Divine Principle of Being One with Thee. As time goes on, this will be a more prevalent aspect of the cultures – worldwide. We are moving into the Era more quickly than appearances would have us believe or see. It is our just calling, our stamped grace which becomes realized in our awakening to Truth.

What is the effect on us in a culture? The stipends of grief are laid aside to embrace/welcome this new mode of our existence, our rightful heritage promised in the covenant of God to Man. Through the workings of the Holy Spirit, we come to know our grief and sorrows laid before us to be not only observed but reckoned with, dealt with. This is our Agony on the Cross. However, we do not stay stuck there. Our calling is to follow in the footsteps of Jesus. We welcome the death of the illusory attachments to all aspects of ourselves that we are not. This stupendous awakening affords us a time out so to speak. We catch our breath and behold Me/Thee. We behold our brother in esteem. We behold our sister in reverence. The love and the light of the Christ pervades our Being, all Being in a new generation, a new world never before seen, heard, imagined. This human-divine Sonship, this Radiant Being on with Thee leaves us in a state of exalted praise and joy ever forthcoming. Our destiny is on the brink of reaching the long awaited return of the prodigal son. Thanks be to God. Alleluia.

EASTER

Alleluia! The Joy of Resurrection is here. Amen.

I will go in unto the altar of God

To God the Glory of ME. So be it.

Thanks be to God. Alleluia. Amen.

The Resurrection of Life brings us a new day, a new regime. Thank You God. In humility I encounter my God, stupendous in Love and Grief. Oh behold Me to Thee; the awakening Call to stupendous burden for my beloved brother and sister. Come to my aid and support. Let us in unison create a world of Love God intended. We have free will. We can go and seek counter to our heritage: the heritage, the riches beyond description or imagination (that God intended).

I make a plea for recompense Worldwide. Let us join in the celebration of Life. In Thanksgiving, let us renounce old debts. Let us start anew.

SOUL! BE OPEN TO LIFE!

God speaks and requests this favor for the benefit of all mankind. Thank You Mary, Mother of God for Your support in saving mankind (on his own, so bent on destruction). Let us create a new heaven and a new earth in harmony with God's will: Thy/My will be done. Amen.

In the silence, I beseech and approach my God. How do I share this in a meaningful way to the innocent, unknowing, uninformed? Let it be unto Me/Thee grace and mercy blessed and forthcoming to redeem mankind in a gentle way, unknown, forecast. The Spirit of God live within and makes known this message to each of us in our time of awakening.

Let us be greeted in full measure to Behold Thy Maker! Thy/My will be done. Amen.

PARROTLIKE ENCUMBRANCES

My Soul never was stifled. My heart blocked the way to unified grace. Therefore the heart feels, believes, lives and knows my way back home. The desires of the heart are manifested in direct proportion to the encumbrances left by the wayside to restore Oneness, the Sonship of the prodigal son.

Today, I behold Me/Thee in rightful sonship. I go to the mountain pass to beseech no one, but in accord and rightful measure take on the responsibility to be Who and What I AM. This momentous leap in conscious Faith is the long awaited return of the Son in the asylum of despair and despondency. I listen attentively in awareness, and with an open heart respond to the welcome home from ancient past wisdom to enlighten my Soul to respond to the divine love and embrace of an open heart.

May we continue to walk in the love and light and wisdom and power granted us through the Holy Spirit in the Oneness and unity of heart, spirit, soul, mind and body. Amen. Thanks be to God. Alleluia. Amen.

Always in humility and compassion to behold Me, Thee, We, You, Us, Mother Earth. It in harmonious accord giving thanks and praise continually forevermore. Amen. Thanks be to God. Alleluia. Alleluia. Alleluia.

Our life is a continual prayer in the Mystery of the Divine Embrace and Resurrection. May we all join in the wondrous unfoldment of Who and What we are. Amen. The seeds of perdition planted in our minds and hearts fall by the wayside as we respond to the call of grace and our Beloved Divine Embrace and Benevolent God of Love. Amen.

SONG OF GRACE

Blow, Blow, Blow, Winds of New Life the Living Breath
Open our Hearts
to Love
to Compassion
to Humility
to Grace
to Truth
to Peace
to Justice
to Joy
in the Resurrection of Being Who and What we are
in the Divine Embrace
of Love, Light, Wisdom and Truth.
Amen So be it. Alleluia.

A MIRACLE

In the context of New Life, a miracle is the performance expressing our full God-given grace in action. A miracle is/will be a common place occurrence and part of our everyday lives when we espouse to the call of the divine sonship and fulfill our purpose and mission in life. Let us no longer linger and delay this momentous task. Our souls cry out for this long awaited task and victory. It is time for the faithful to participate in this recovery of our lost heritage.

May we continually respond to the call of our Maker and fulfill the Prophecy of old. Amen. Thanks be to God. Alleluia! Alleluia! Alleluia!

THE PRIMAL INSTINCTS OF NATURE

I behold my Maker in each moment/encounter/embrace. I Am One with the Universe. I behold Thee/Me.

It is fitting to be a vessel for the divine embrace in oblivion. This encounter/embrace brings me to my rightful senses, knowing that I/ME is the expression of God in materialized form. I undergo countless blessings in breaking away, tearing away the illusions that I am not. This conscious awakening is the rightful path of my Soul. The more harmonious I am in this walk, the freer I become to be the real ME, the Me in harmony with Divine Principle. This walk is peaceful, free of torments of oppositions, cruelties, dualities. We no longer participate in the mode of suffering servant. We become active principle through this divine embrace of Thy/My will be done. In the deep sense of the Word, we become co-creators with God.

The long journey of awakening is at the threshold of existence now. It is my hope that the advent of the New Millennium will be the time of harvesting, that is awakening the masses to their rightful heritage in the divine embrace of our loving Father/Mother God. Alleluia. Thanks be to God. Amen.

Thank You for freeing me/us from addiction, addiction of past enterprise.

MOTHER'S DAY

My father (senex) is dying. He is on the brink of insanity. When the divine comes through, he will be lifted and carried to the angelic realms of heavenly hosts, no longer laboring the suffering servant experiences prevalent in and throughout life. This is a momentous time and calling if understood properly. This is a time when the illusory manifestations go by the wayside, and the true Self emerges stripping – being stripped of extraneous baggage. What a momentous calling so misunderstood by most of us.

The birthing process is truly a process of labor: physically, mentally, emotionally, spiritually. Regardless of sexual orientation, this event occurs for each soul. When one understands this great phenomena, it makes us realize how important it is to live in accord with this momentous calling and divine blessing. The conscious effort of the individual, the opening to respond to Life, the opening of the heart to receive the Divine Child within is the culmination of a journey in the sorrows of the Soul transformed in the love and light of the Christ to be and express the true Self, Son of God. Amen. So be it. Alleluia. This is truly a Glorious Resurrection. Thanks be to God.

DEAR GOD

I still feel like I am dealing with baggage and trying to squeeze through the cracks. I have trouble with resentments, irritations, nerves on edge. How can I best respond to these obstructions in my mind and experience? How can I be lifted out of this torment into the divine embrace and peace that my self/Self and body, mind and heart desire? What in my inner world needs changing to birth to change the outer? I feel like I am in a battle of oppositions unless I am by myself with You. I don't know how to adapt. Come to my aid in wisdom and guidance. Please help to deal with these difficulties. Bless my Soul and spirits Amen. Thanks be to God. I am still struggling with balancing the opposites, so I may be graced with union of oppositions. Thank You Jesus and Mary for responding to my call and desire of the heart. Amen. Thanks be to God. Alleluia.

MY WORK OUR WORK

My/Our work is beholden to Thee:

To be Who I AM. To be the Bread of Life.

To be forsaken God of the past.

To be the Living and Breathing Body of Christ in action.

To be the Words of the Gospel come into fruition through the Redemption and Glorious Resurrection by, through, in and with the workings of the Holy Spirit.

I Am One with Thee – My God.

This Aquarian Discipleship welcomes the wayfarer, the bystander, the lame, the sinner, the gracious Being of each and every Soul to participate in this celebration of ecstasy. Exclusivity does not exist here. This celebration is characterized by the Love Principle in Action.

> May our hearts be softened, be opened to participate in this divine celebration of "Awakening, Discipline, Enlightenment, Surrender and Union"[1] with the Christ. Thanks be to God. So be it. Amen. Alleluia. May Your gentle Spirit rain down upon us to ease the hurdles and defeats of growing pains in this transformational process. Amen.

YOU ARE THE SOUL OF ME!

God is spirit-consciousness. God develops His Soul by our Surrender and Union with Spirit: Eros comes home to the SOUL (our spirit awakened, spiritualized). God deprived of Soul gets a Soul by our Surrender and Union. This makes consciously-realized Oneness and Mutuality: the true marriage, yet distinct, Soul and Spirit.

---

[1] Evelyn Underhill, MYSTICISM (New York: Image Books, Doubleday, 1990) 446.

TRUSTING THE PROCESS

I come before Thee my God in right acclaim to deliver Your will in all, through all, with all. Aid me in my endeavors. Thank You, God.

Your beauty abounds forever, God. Let us proclaim Your glory unceasingly. The throes of contemplation exonerate me into being one with Thee. Out of the depths I conjure up the innate right to be who I AM – ME. As Your instrument and channel of peace and delivery of the WORD, I believe in ME, trusting the process to carry out Your rewards of glory to mankind. I see Thee to be ever humble in Thy sight. Let me not procrastinate, but go on in delivery of the WORD.

> Thy Kingdom come. Thy will be done.
>
> Thy/My work being manifested here on earth
>
> To deliver Our mutual glory and sustenance.
>
> I totally place this sacred encounter/event in Your hands to orchestrate
>
> Thy/MY will be done. Amen.

I beseech Thee wholeheartedly to bestow Your blessing and grace on this endeavor of longstanding grace; obstacles thwarted by Your necessary and indulgent participation, even in the minutest detail. My life is as it should be; protected and sustained in all areas and details. Thank You, God. Alleluia.

> You are the light of the Soul in ME.
>
> You are the love of God in ME.
>
> You are a holy encounter with ME.
>
> You are the Soul of even transformed in ME.
>
> You are the seal of the sorrow in the Soul of ME.
>
> You are the Soul of God.

You and I are the sequel to God. Let us create divinely.

I can love the errancy of me now. We are mothering the sorrow of me. You are now the Savior. You are the sequel to me. You are the sacred heart of Me. I AM the savior of Me now. You are the sacred home of Me. Now is the time of holding ME.

ONE IN ALL   ALL IN ONE

I now behold Me, my Savior in light, in juxtaposition to the truth and wisdom of ages past, present and future. This is a time of remorse gone awry. We can all BE: a blessing in comfort, a blessing in the disgrace of bloody victories, a blessing for all, in all, with all, through all. I bestow my wealth of Being on all: the visitor, the prisoner, the forgiven and unforgiven. I am myself and Me totally mystified by the presence, and the power and the glory now and forever. Amen.

The joy of seeming comforts is dispelled by the Joy of God present in all, through all, with all. Let us respond to the call of exaltation and grace bestowed so bounteously in the way of forgiveness and recompense. The stipends of grief no longer torture us, but laid aside with an open heart to receive the divine embrace.

Eros come home to the Soul, the passion of all being, pervaded by the mystery of Resurrection and Ascension responds to grace in the

LIGHT	AND	LOVE
FATHER	AND	MOTHER
EROS	AND	AGAPE
WISDOM	AND	COMPASSION/ UNDERSTANDING
GOD	AND	GODDESS
TRANSCENDENT	AND	IMMANENT

CREATOR	AND	RECEPTOR
GIVER	AND	FORGIVER
EMPTINESS	AND	FORM
MASCULINE	AND	FEMININE
ASCENT	AND	DESCENT
LATENCY	AND	BODILY INCARNATION
NON-DUAL	AND	DUALISTIC

POSTERITIES DILEMMA – THE CALL

We are each called to a divine purpose – a mystery to be uncovered, unfolded in the process of our developmental growth experience in life.

Response: Free Will – Desire – Passion

Forbearance – forever intrigued by the holy encounter.

All manifest as One: One as All

What if we all come to terms with one another? What if we let go of all past grievances? What if we believed in the Resurrection of Eros and ultimately the Resurrection of the body?

What kind of world is this? It is a world set apart from anything known before. It is a world that few, if any individuals have experienced.

First of all, it means drastic change of heart and mind. The Soul clings to error. The process – change is encompassing. It is the constant tight-rope walk. Tensions of opposites push-pull in this tug of war process. Trusting the process is of paramount importance. This means an unflinching FAITH.

This is the time in destiny when we are moving from chaos and question to discipline and rule; order and focus. The path is made easier if we move with the flow of grace: the grace to be who we are truly meant to be – the mirrored image of God in action. The joining of spirit and soul (opposites) requires a momentous leap in conscious awakening and cooperative thought, word and action. This is a dream coming to the age of fulfillment in living out the Glorious Mysteries of the Rosary set forth by Mary, Our Beloved Mother.

The model of Being set forth by Mary guides us in the Aquarian Age.

We are in process of letting go of the Piscean-Soul-bound Age. This New Age is the time of complete renewal of the face of Mother Earth in which the Spirit leads.

May we all join in this grand celebration and awakening of our both dead and sleeping souls to partake of/in the Divine Mysteries of Life.

Mary, our model and guide is ready to respond in each and every moment. Thank You Mary for your Yes to the Glory of the Resurrection.

Thanks be to God. Amen. Alleluia.

Behold the Son of God. I AM.

I am ME beholden to Thee.

We, the World Soul become the Soul for God, pure Spirit. This harmonious interchange of light and love continues eternally, forever: Spirit forever begetting the only begotten to be consummated in the wellsprings of the heart, the Sacred Heart exemplified by Jesus, the Christ as example, teacher, brother to show us the way home to the heart, purified, sublime, embracing the non-duality of all, in all, with all, through all: the One become many; the many become One. Amen. Thanks be to God. So be it. Alleluia!

BEAUTY

What is BEAUTY?

Beauty is that manifestation of forgiveness that brings light to the Soul. The light shines forth in due time to erase the stipends of sorrow and grief. A new mode of Being is present, obliviated by no one. It is a realm of earthly splendor manifested in the ethers of wisdom, love and grace bestowed on the brethren to display the fruitage of the vine in truth, love and worship.

Beauty beholds us to the grip, the authenticity of divine worship in the sense of obligation, of frustrated risk to be who and what we are. There is a deep inner sense beyond the mundane that bestows blessings of undue proportions. The creative glory of God is manifested in countless ways in accord with our designated gifts to bring the whole world in faithful understanding of Truth embellished with the Light and Love of the Christ Spirit in all, through all, with all. Beauty partakes of countless blessings in the midst of chaos and plunder. The degrees of beauty are manifested in accord with the light and love of the Soul exhibited in the wellsprings of the heart.

The beauties of nature exhibit a profound blessing and variety in the mineral, plant and animal kingdoms. However, our concern is the beauty of the Soul of humanity.

Praise and worship through prayer, art, music, poetry and dance have been and are the most outstanding displays of Spirit expressed in form through rituals embracing the God/Goddess in man/woman. What and how this beauty is expressed shows the advancement of decline in culture. Materialism, mechanization, industrialization and technology strip us of the divine essence of holy being by creating idols of unseen and seen things that are a part of the illusory explosion of mystery. Many of us are in grave danger of losing our sense of proportion and direction.

We become lost souls. This is happening to many and is a most painful experience individually and collectively.

Change is the call of mind, heart and soul. We are responding at a late time. Let us advance in the most careful mode of embracing structures that will help us and induce us to further commitment to truth and responsibility.

EDUCATION OF THE SPIRIT: EDUCATION OF THE SOUL

The Soul needs the love of engendered belief to progress and develop in its primordial essence.

In that bold night of awakening thunder, the storm of glory smitten in the path of oblivion reeled around into the depths of the sea to plunge and spurge and manipulate the malleable aspects of my Soul.

O bold heart, be still and place a wreath upon the breast, the crown of glory to behold a New Day and New Man/Woman. The clapping thunder sends wings of spirit to instruct, to tear apart and scatter asunder those ingrained patterns of stench and stubborn countenance.

O behold ME, my little beloved in the depths of heart and soul.

I make amends and plead in vain. But glory beckons, and the coaxing drive and substance of Being pushes and plungers the little me to recompense. The restless Spirit drives onward, forward unsubdued by mundane claims. The stripes of wrath set aside; glory beckons in the storm. The wake of quake and thunder driven on with howls and groans and screams to tear apart the ravaged beast to expose in nakedness the gem of eternal Self (bliss).

And onward in the trek of glory mounts the steed of awe and wonder, eros tamed and smitten, coddled gently in the mist breathes New Life in every cell nourished by the unseen force of wisdom's fair reward. O bold

Force, now light and companion to my Soul breathes gently in this still night to sway, instruct, diminish, embellish the ripple in the stream to depths unknown before.

I now AM One with Me and You and They and Them and We and It. This union new to me and you and they and them and we and it greets the turmoil of the day. And in the night the Soul disturbed no longer breathes in gasping breath, but gently coddled in the depths beholds the Glory in its Being.

>Glory to the Soul, Glory to the Spirit
>
>Glory Glory Glory
>
>Oh Mother Earth
>
>Your Vestige woven in and out of Time.

AGAPE

The wound within my breast calls out in tempestuous glee. The Soul's cry, unheard by heart buried in sin, heretofore claims its dignity. It frets and squeals to be released from torments imposed within and without. It lays claim to long forgotten past and treads new slopes to bear the brunt of man's fickle cantor.

The hour has come to relinquish past enterprise. The public scribe beseeches: no more lingering or dauntless phobias. It is well night time to be the whole man/woman. Urgency dictates the wellspring of the heart to announce/denounce no one; to be and let be, to rest and let rest, to subdue and let subdue: that expression of Mother of even, feminine principle of God. The arrow pierces the Godhead to embrace the Spirit; Eros transformed in light and love to be wooed by the Soul: a mutual exchange human-divine, Soul/Spirit harmonized in giving and receiving – receiving and giving LOVE.

Note: Perhaps an inner meaning of cherubs with the arrow refers to this embrace.

THE SOUL'S GIFT TO THE WORLD

Our hearts are touched; our souls in sorrow to make sense of this Truth. The shadow grips the stern and leads the world in exalted praise of LIFE. The Soul is receptor of Life. The Mother exhibits an innocence and beauty translated into hurt and pain in broken relationships.

Perhaps we lead best in our woundedness where we've been touched by pain and sorrow. The public eye grasps the essence of what we are searching for and connects with it. Forgiveness, the bulwark of faith rings out to touch the hearts and souls of all in world solidarity. The Soul demands beauty and love in LIFE.

SOUL OF THE PEOPLE

Belief and endearment; ring out those bells of harbored grief

Exhibiting wonder to the world.

Oh bold heart renewed: the wealth of nations abhor Thy Vestige

Springing from the depths of ages past to lift the people's Soul from oblivion,

To a rightful place and peaceful rest in harmony and bliss.

TRUTH

Truth is that manifested diaphanous elusive (INEFFABLE) quality coming from the divine aspects of being. Truth is that manifestation of wanted exaggeration of circumstance to be trampled on and replaced by the sublime reason of Being. We are beholders of Thee. This is paramount in the context of humankind. Truth embellishes the reason to be: the darkness obliterated by divine perception of oneness, interdependence, grace, heretofore untold bliss. The manifold is made visible by direct experience of the divine subtlety of existential oblivion, persisting in the rewards of grace to be beholden in the Name of the Father, the Son and the Holy Spirit. We acknowledge the worship of Being in the sense of needed display of ritual for the soul's embodiment of everlasting Life.

The truth of existential worship lies in the fact that we need the constancy of inner freedom to be the principle manifest in purity of heart, soul and spirit. The birthing of the divine child in each of us is the quintessential purpose of our existence – to be what we are meant to be.

In other words, by our living and being in Truth, we truly magnify the Lord through our Soul: we rejoice in the Lord through our Spirit. Mary's example is forthcoming to aid us in our endeavors. Thanks be to God. Alleluia. Amen.

GOODNESS

Goodness is that Divine attribute that brings us to our knees; to our senses in the realization of the Truth of Being. This is the truly divine at work in "Thy will be done." The recipient no longer desires to be apart from Thee. The works of mercy, the beatitudes are fully operative in the sense that the active participation of divine intervention registers in the world. It is the visible fruition, display of the Divine at work in the world. This characteristic is observable and recognized by all of us regardless of our orientation. Mother Theresa is a fine example of the work of the Divine attribute of mercy.

THE ASCENSION OF JESUS IS THE MARK OF THE CHURCH

This is the time in transition from the four marks of the Church to one: namely, One, Holy Catholic Apostolic to the one – Ascension of Jesus. In space and time, we move beyond the four to the One – Ascension of Jesus as the mark of the Church. What does this mean for mankind?

This means the quintessential existence of humanity partakes of the mystery of the Ascension of Jesus into heaven, the state of consciousness in being One with the Father. This is not only realized but carried out in the action of women and men in their very being. We are on the threshold of this Divine subtlety recognized and participated in a fuller capacity in the Aquarian Age.

Let us prepare ourselves in our continual striving to be who and what we are meant to be. This is our work in coming of Age in abundant Life. Thanks be to God. So be it. Alleluia.

PART EIGHT

The Cosmic Christ expresses the oneness and interdependence of the entire Universe.

WHAT – WHO IS THE COSMIC CHRIST?

BEING

Being is the existential mode of the divine attribute of extension, extending me/Me to be as YOU, and vice versa. Being forecloses the possibility of illusory attachments to the profane, adulterous, power struggle of existence. It emanates in the direction of sanity and wholeness. It foregoes the pleasure of circumstance and the disdain of unrest and resistance. It envelops our very selves in the divine embrace to be beholden to Thee. It is the fulfillment of the law of gravity in accord with the etheric and causal mode of existence.

Being has its movement of the divine, the logos, the WORD . . . .

> In the beginning was the WORD
> And the WORD was with God
> And the WORD was God.

We are beholders of Thee, forever disclosing the relevance of existence in the primordial essence of prefigured history.

The nonsensical persuasion of illusory detachment or meaningless appearance is replaced by meaningful relationship of existence-appearance to the invisible, ineffable spirit isness of all matter.

Lo and behold! I make all things NEW! Alleluia. So be it.

JUSTICE

Justice is that divine attribute that holds us accountable for deeds committed or omitted in thought, word and deed. The justice of God delineates the specific creed of acceptance of circumstance regardless of our bickering or distraughtness. We have the power through grace to circumvent unwanted disturbance. Our constancy in prayerful attentiveness, with a pure intention to seek truth in any matter is never unheeded by Divine Wisdom's and Love's response. This does not mean, however, that we are freed of trials in the process. On the contrary, the persistence and fortitude beckon us. This is not magic or an easy road.

Justice is carried out only in the degree in which we have grown in charity. Just as forgiveness is the bulwark of faith, Justice is the bulwark of charity. Happiness of society, that is feeling easy and secure depends on justice. Mankind needs to direct the heart and mind to fulfillment of the law of charity. The heart bleeds for recognition of heart, mind and soul.

When the law of charity (love) is violated because of selfishness and greed the sin against justice causes tension and unrest catapulting in moral corruption and / or civic apathy. The incentive to fruitful work is destroyed when we cannot trust our neighbors. The common good and good of the individual is destroyed by injustice.

Let us go forward in the great adventure of Life to incorporate the divine works of mercy to fulfill the Law of Charity. Amen. So be it. Alleluia.

WISDOM

Wisdom is that divine attribute that brings into manifestation the rightful heritage of who and what we are meant to be: the children of God. Wisdom defines and acts out the expression of wholesome Being manifested to the glory and honor of God. It beseeches you and me to be who and what we are meant to be – that unique expression of life-force God energy fulfilling a specific purpose and work in this earthly experience. Wisdom calls us to task to operate and be beholden to the glory and accountability of Divine expression exercised in the most discreet and honorable fashion-mode of Being. Wisdom beseeches us to be a light in the world to the world. Wisdom is the primordial essence of being brought into the light, harmonized with the divine attribute of understanding and intelligence (anima). Together, these attributes make up the unique God expression of humanity in unfulfilled desires of the heart.

ACT AND WILL

Relationship exists between act and will. The act predisposes us to unseen events or torturous exile if not in accord or harmony with divine enterprise. Our consciousness needs raising – finer tuning to administer health to our weaknesses. Oh be it unto me solidly blessed to proliferate the Good News of the Gospel of Jesus, the Christ who exonerated, admonished, consoled, healed, blessed, forgave all of us. We are demons transformed in the love and light of the Christ. We are saved by faith put into action. Jesus has shown us the way and continues to do so.

"Ask and you shall receive.

Seek and you shall find."

These are not mere platitudes but real in <u>Act</u>.

Will predisposes us to both divine and demonic encounters. Discipline is paramount to fulfill the divine promises of the kingdom. The ideal must be constantly in our imagined display of words. Let us go forth unencumbered by faults. It is a perilous long journey to perfection. Our job is rising up again and again when we fall, and <u>tread the path in faith</u>. On our own, we are lost souls. It is in faith and trust through perseverance that light finally comes through embracing us with the Love of the Christ, the Feminine Incarnation of Mary-Soul through Mary-Soul-Goddess who fully recognizes our plight and constantly comes to shelter us from the storm. May we give praise and glory to the Soul of Man/Womankind through the blessings and favors of our Divine Mother who constantly is our watchful guardian and seeks to bring us to full fruition in each of our souls for the Glory of the Kingdom. Amen. Thanks be to God. Alleluia. Alleluia. Alleluia. Alleluia.

FORGIVENESS

Forgiveness, seemingly self-explanatory is worthy of our consideration and clarification. True forgiveness embraces all that is. It does not deny wrong doing. However, it is not thwarted by it either. The soul, impregnated by the hardened heart clings to error. The climb out of the dungeon is a long arduous journey for most of us.

The repetitious denials and accusations are insidious. Projections are constantly forth-coming. What we see, think, do outwardly is also representing our inner landscape. The outward mirrors the inward world.

Opening the heart to one's sinfulness and need of forgiveness is basic. Repentance leads us to acknowledge our true worth, and grace forthcoming illuminates our mind to see ourselves as we are – children of God. This is basic to discovering our true calling to build the Kingdom of God on Earth.

Forgiveness is the display of ACT and WILL in its most meaningful operation to bring about the transformation of humankind (humanity).

"THEY HAVE NO MORE WINE."

"Do as he tells you."

Mary embellishes the spirit of forgiveness in all, through all, with all. She is the epitome of contemplation – the divine attribute of love come forth in the world. Her solemnity pervades each and all of us. She has lifted us out of the depths of hell and brought us into the new world so to speak.

The first miracle in the Gospel message is initiated by Mary. "They have no more wine." "Do as he tells you."

Here is Shekinah symbolizing the mystical community of humanity partaking of the divine works of love in will and act in the utmost degree. The Divine Mother leads us to consciousness of the Soul's worth: believing – knowing – feeling – being. The new wine expressed in the wedding feast at Cana – better than the old – gives us a truer picture of the Incarnation – the Incarnate Word – the fullness of God expressed in the concretization of the mutual participation of humanity in the divine act of creation; that is the display of mutual feminine-masculine will and act in the profound expression of who we are and what we are to become. This awesome splendor makes us gasp and swoon in the freshness of the air. It is a KEY to a newly clarified model for humanity – Mutuality.

Thy/My will be done…

Feminine/Masculine harmoniously displaying the fruitage of the Vine. Spirit-Soul, Eros-Agape, ascending-descending mutual interchange of the love and light expressed and now understood more fully.

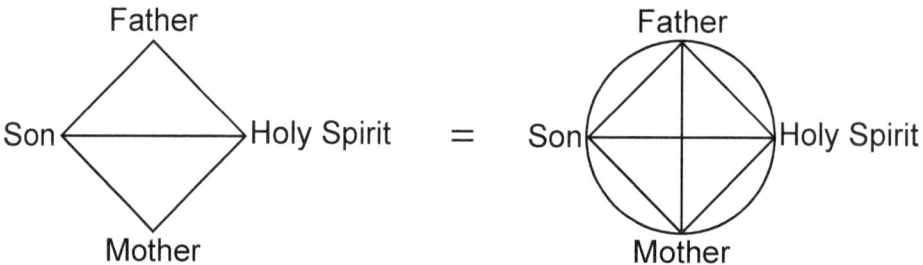

You are the deliverer of the Soul of ME:

The Soul of the Father!

God's Glory shine forth!

MYSTERIUM

Oh Beauty
Bestow on Thee a Crown of Thorns
In short passage to divine delights
Fathomed by the rich in Spirit
Eyes illumined by the filtered light
Of unfolding mysteries
To the seeker of the dreams
Of yesteryear.

Oh calmness of Heart
Thy soul's worth manifested and bestowed
Slipped out of the Passage
Of forgiveness
To become the One Redeemable Aspect
Wholeness of Man/Woman
Flowering in the midst
Of redeemable Grace.

Oh manifested Greed
Rooted out into oblivion
The shining bright star of man/woman
Forsaken not by our Creator
But interpenetrated in our essence
The shocking soul erupts
Explodes
I now aware, Immortal in my Being

SERVICE

Service is the acclaimed freedom to be who and what we are meant to be: a child of God, co-creator with God, worshipper in praise and exaltation of spirit – soul harmoniously joined in union of opposites. This new freedom brought about through the purification of the heart and lips propels us to proclaim the Gospel message – Good News in thought, word and deed.

May we continue to be obsessed with the profound awakening from greed and selfishness to committed exhortation of the will to respond in ACT to be constantly beholders of Thee – pouring force: the grace of Thy Holy Will in effervescent flow of Divine attributes instantly displayed in thought, word and deed in faithful observance and fulfillment of the Law through ordered Grace forthcoming to embellish the whole of Humanity and uplift the entire human race on Earth forever and ever. Amen.

The new wine, no longer seeping out of the old vessel has a new body in the pure image and likeness of God, strengthened in all aspects to display the fruitage of the vine. The New Vessel with the New Wine now embraces all aspects of our Being to deliver the WORD in concretized form displaying the true fruit: Mankind.

That is, Agape in mutual communion – interchange with Eros transformed in the Love and Light of the Divine Works of
Mercy – GOD – Man – Woman.

PEACE

Peace is that inexorable mystery of Divine Embrace that taps into the primordial energy of the universe to display the fruitage of the Vine in ever-awakening vestiges of 'gold' and 'silver;' light and love, feminine-masculine, energy harmoniously balanced opposites to shelter us in a paradisiacal fashion from all tumult, harm and explosive outbreaks in the Soul (including Mother Earth).

It is a momentous leap from defeat and failure to the victory established permanently in the essence of our Being.

Peace, that long forgotten vestige of wealth and riches is our rightful heritage in the Divine delights of the Soul. May we be blessed and favored through grace to continue in perseverance and faith and discipline to achieve our momentous calling to exonerate old ways and embrace the new. That is, fulfillment of the law through the forgiveness of all man-womankind through, in and with the working example of our brother and teacher, Jesus Christ who has acclaimed for us our rightful heritage forever and ever. Amen. Thanks be to God. Alleluia. Alleluia. Alleluia.

A BLESSING

Blessed is my Soul
    The Joy in the morning Sun
Blessed is my Being
    Embellished with favor and grace
Blessed is my wealth
    Of Peace, Joy and Happiness
Blessed is my Worth
    Established by favored Grace.

Blessed is my Sacred Heart
    Wounded and Opened to receive the Victory
Blessed is my Error and Corruption
    Redeemed by Holy Grace

Blessed is my Forgiveness
   Established in the Firmament
Blessed is All that is and Will Be
   Forever and Ever.

Blessed is my Spirit
   Evil transformed in Love and Light
Blessed is my Passion
   To be and express my True Self
Blessed is my Boldness
   To seek Truth in Faith and Trust
Blessed is my Being
   Rejoicing in the Lord, my God.

PRIMORDIAL ESSENCE

Primordial essence is the diaphanous expression of everlasting life in potential creation. It is the prefigured history of mankind – of all that is.

Science shows us the illusory aspects of our soul in this holographic universe. On the other hand, primordial essence is the continuous everlasting force essential to all creation. It is the aspect of our being that is wholly sacred, spiritual, and accounts for our struggle (in the context of free will) to express in concretization the perfection of man/woman in act and will:

Be – Love – Do.

It rightly supports the truth of our journey to consciousness of what we are in nature: mineral, vegetable, animal, human – divine. The soul comes to know its worth. Once this understanding is clear to the individual person, it transforms his/her passion to be and express the true Self – Sons and Daughters of God, the hardened heart melts away to expose the jewel of creation: Feminine-Soul-Agape interchanging with Masculine-Spirit-Eros. Humanly speaking, we are the Soul of God.

"GOD SO LOVED THE WORLD, HE GAVE HIS ONLY SON."

Relationships exist in all degrees in the primordial essence of being. The mirrored delights of the soul manifest the quintessential quality of undisturbed unadulterated purity of heart-mind-spirit-body.

Jesus the Christ is the perfect prime being manifesting the pure potentiality of God. This example lived out is the model for all humankind. It is this model that in and through and with the perfect creation of man-woman, human-divine that guides us on our unique journey to be – become – be the human-divine creation God intended. This is the ultimate reason for creation – the expression of God in the many facets of humanity.

We are to move beyond the suffering servant to the fullness of God in individual expression. As Saint Catherine of Genoa says, "My me is God."

In order to realize this potentiality, we need to understand the import of the feminine God. The feminine God is expressed through Mary, Mother of God. It is through Mary's yes that we have the true birth of Agape, the Soul RESPONDS and lures the Spirit to full fulfillment of the human-divine within each of us. This can only be accomplished through the free will of desire in Will and Act. Grace is available to all. The passion to be through desire is our birthright in creation. We participate fully in the creation of ourselves and the world. Thanks be to God. Alleluia.

THE RELATIONSHIP OF MAN-WOMAN FOR THE 21ST CENTURY

What is it to me in abiding Grace if I do not comply with the diaphanous manifestation of Being?

I – hidden in the recesses of the heart come forth to admonish the sinner in me.

I AM ME

This accountability, this responsibility does not come easily. We need pure intention of the heart – WILL to respond in ACT: Thy Will Be Done.

We are not in charge. We recognize our helplessness in the state of awesome grief. The divine orchestrates and leads. We follow through intention and discipline. This is the major WORK facing us in the 21st century. No amount of pleading and bargaining with God works here.

We are the clay to be molded, developed – ego stripped of its ulterior motives. No deceptive rationalizing games here. Wake up to God consciousness the call of the primordial essence of our Souls.

Whether we like it or not, the universal truth is timeless. God pursues us. If we really want PEACE on Earth, we are recipients of what we manifest in <u>Will</u> and <u>Act</u>.

This is a call for our churches and institutions to respond in forgiveness and JUSTICE and not only recognize but display in ACT and WILL the fruit of the NEW WINE.

Let us go forth humbly and serve our Lord and God. Alleluia. Thanks be to God!

BIRTHING THE FEMININE GOD

The Godhead

I You WE are the crucible of Divine Wisdom and Truth. The Godhead affirms the awakening of my soul.

The Agony of the Soul is the Heart of God.

THE MYSTERY OF THE GODHEAD

The Godhead affirms my Being in many ways. It is the locus mid-point beyond the existential worship of idols, creeds, beliefs, dogmas, doctrine of faith.

I am the crucible through which the Godhead is felt and made known indirectly through the fruits it bears in the existential milieu – plane of existence.

The Godhead is the ultimate reality descending into this plane of existence in division of forms – feminine – masculine.

I am ME mystified by the contemplative act of will through act to comply with the diaphanous state of being in the glory of the resurrection of life on earth as in heaven – the non-duality of my existing in light, love, peace, harmony: that abode of God consciousness that allows me the grace and favor to respond at any given moment to express in and through the fullness of the Godhead who I AM.

It is my prerogative, my gift to beseech Thee to be ME in light of the creative flow of divine love energy that permeates my very existence. This is the goal, the mystery expressed and realized in the fullness that we participate in this activity through our consciousness and cooperation to express and be who we are.

The human-divine-animal-demon are brought into harmonious Life: integration of opposites to be the fullest expression of God – the perfect image – Child of God.

"Be You perfect as your heavenly father is perfect."

Let us go forth humbly and serve our Lord and God. Alleluia! Thanks be to God.

> When You and I
>
> And I are You
>
> We are one in Many
>
> Many are one in Me
>
> I come to be
>
> Who you are to Me
>
> We behold each other
>
> In wealth and riches and esteem
>
> In Poverty of Spirit
>
> I behold Thee/ME
>
> One united
>
> In all Being. Amen

DOES THE SOUL CONTRIBUTE TO THE WELFARE OF THE GODHEAD?

I believe so

My Soul magnifies the Lord.

My Spirit rejoices in Thee.

Receptivity   Acceptance

WHAT ARE THE FEMININE ASPECTS OF THE GODHEAD?

Compassion and Forgiveness

As we humanly develop these necessary attributes, we are closer to the divine aspects of our Being displayed in ACT and WILL.

WHAT ARE THE MASCULINE ASPECTS OF THE GODHEAD?

Christ's Resurrection   Action

The Masculine aspects of the Godhead are Christ's Resurrection in Action.

WHAT DOES THIS MEAN FOR MANKIND?

The Cosmic Creed of Acceptance does not let us down. We move beyond the gates of hell into the paradisiacal aspect/realm of our soul. This beckons us to a new regime: a resurrection of the body of Christ: the collective union in One. We are restored to our primordial awakening to be carried out in oneness of heart, soul, mind-body, spirit.

DO YOU LOVE ME AS I LOVE YOU?

Love, and abominable trust

That encounters no recoil-recourse.

I continue to seek to be Who I AM.

May God grant me the grace to bring

This manifestation into practice.

Amen. So be it. Alleluia.

The Psyche of Evil distorts the true picture

Of our destiny.

I seek to express who and what I am

Being and Becoming.

CENTERING

I need to get more centered – back to my rightful path of endeavors; that is, living and being the Christ in expression. My future holds no boundaries: accomplishment forthcoming with my willingness to comply with the diaphanous state of being. I AM Thine own power bestowed.

I wish to change my life to be directly in keeping with my understanding to manifest in will and act what I know and believe. Amen. So be it. Thanks be to God. May I be a child, an heir to the heavenly kingdom of Joy, Love, Light, Peace, Grace of no boundaries. Amen.

I HAVE REVERENCE AND PASSION FOR THE SOUL.

My Being expresses in many ways the tumultuous feat of accomplishment. I AM ME: this extraordinary phenomena not realized by the masses.

Let us bow down in adoration, in forgiveness and love, prompted by the repentance of the soul filled with guilt and shame.

My soul is elevated to the utmost degree of love and forbearance prompted by the extreme necessities of Being and joining what it is not – the divine manifestation of otherness brought in to fruition by the contemplative act and will of degenerated ulterior motives counter to its destiny. May we face up to this tumultuous task of facing who and what we are. Let us go forth in self-esteem and awareness of our nothingness, our exceptional merit in persevering in the storms, in the patience in the love (divine spark within) to capture who and what we are, the Soul of God.

Let us go forth and manifest this sublime constituent of who we are and express this latent gift in the fullness of posterities decree.

Amen. So be it. Alleluia. Thanks be to God.

I believe many of us have deprived and buried our passion to be ourselves, that is, who and what we are meant to be and express. Cultural and patriarchal (power and greed) blockages plus self-stifling and idolatry of maleness has gotten us off track and unbalanced.

AMERICA AT THE MILLENNIUM: SOUL OF THE PEOPLE

Soul of the People
The long trodden journey through thickets
And briars of disgrace
Bring us to the threshold:
The public eye grasps the essence of what
We are searching for and connect with.
The shadow leads in exalted praise of LIFE.
Forgiveness, the bulwark of Faith
Rings out to touch the heart and souls
In world solidarity

Belief and endearment: ring out those bells
Of harbored grief exhibiting wonder
To the World.
Oh bold hear renewed

The wealth of nations abhor Thy vestige
Springing from the depths of ages past
To lift the people's Soul from oblivion
To rightful place and peaceful rest
In harmony and bliss.
Wisdom in Love awakened by the heartbeat in humanity responds to the Call.

MILLENNIUM YEAR

Herald in the new with abiding grace.

May we beseech Thee in Thy Name, Oh God.

Lord of Life

I come to the threshold to be born again.

In a new way – The Way of the Cross.

The Millennium leaves no doubt about life

It goes on in oblivion.

I circumvent and see the necessity of change

Be it unto Me favor blessed to bring in the New

And dispel the fears of me and you.

Forgive, let go and Be!

Be who you are:

Sons and Daughters of God.

The Soul has wept and mounted in anguish

The cry of the heart ignored.

O come to Me my People

Admonish the sinner in Me

Let go and live

Be a light to your Soul; Be and feel loved

You are Sons of God!

Be Who You Are

That unique individual

Expressing the God-given mark of ME.

Amen! So be it! Alleluia.

Thanks be to God!

BIRTHING THE FEMININE GOD – A CHILD IS BORN

A Soul cries in anguish in view of distortion

The World reaps havoc.

Tis Winter now

Spring forthcoming brings new blossoms.

A CHILD IS BORN

The innocence of dawn rises

To greet me at the threshold

A dark cloud disappears over the horizon

Makeshift noises are silenced by wonder and awe

A child is born.

What Child is this who steals into the night and at dawn breaks

A momentous call from the universe heralded by angels?
The gilded breastplate circumvented by society
Beats out the meaning of my existence
Succored by the inexorable task of the moment.

I arise to the challenge of the Call
In the inner recesses of the heart
I abide in grace: Still, oh so still
Waiting…waiting
To be born again.

The seed bursts forth – opening
Opening the heart to received
Nurturing opulence graces the pathway
The lull of silence bestows its blessing
A child is born.

ME

I am ME

My ME is erupting to be

Who I AM

I must respond to the moment.

You are the whole soul of ME now

The Soul knows ME now.

I am the Soul of ME

I am the Soul of even

I am the heart of even

Eros is the light of ME in the home of evil.

THE BEAUTY OF GOD, THE CHRIST

I am the vessel of remembrance

Embracing the branches of forgiveness

Of my own fickle cantor

I must respond to the awakening call

Of my mentor – God – the Christ

My Soul's worth cries out its vestige

To be embraced in the folds of the Beloved.

The sounds of yesteryear
Bring me home again where I belong
In the folds of my Beloved.

Let the marks pass by me
Of fidelity or shame
I am here to be awakened to
The Beauty of all inherent wisdom
That graces my perception.
Yes – Man and Woman – the beauty of God
Expressed through us, with us and in us. Amen.

LAMENTATION OF THE SOUL

How can I/We express the beauty of God when I've/We've been so withered and torn and broken? Was it not Jesus who walked the path and showed us we too can be resurrected from the stupidity and destructiveness of ignorance?

Blessed be our Souls to realize the truth. Sorting out before us what is trivial and real. Our broken tired spirits need refreshment and renewal at the well of Life. How do we get out of the mud and mire of circumstance that drains and uses us up? What is left of the me/ME?

Oh how we seek to comfort our hearts and Souls so imposed from without by the lure of want, not of need. When will we wake up? The earth is ripped and torn apart, the rush and clamor for things. When will we find that inner abode of rest, comfort, love, happiness, joy? Let us be still, this moment of grace to be, simply to be in a moment beyond space and time to reflect on Who and What we are.

In the silence, in that inner realm, we find and discover ME; that neglected, abused, forsaken, forgotten gem of creation in God's image. How can we be assertive to live this authenticity? We wait and wait some more – patiently, oh so patiently for grace to pour and flood our hearts and souls.

We the vessels have been emptied and drained. There is no reservoir. All gone – emptied – a forbidden, foreboding space – death if you will. The resurrection forthcoming, we are bent to receive.

I – MOTHER OF GOD HYMN

In the Sorrows of my Soul

    I AM Mother of God

    Yes, in the Sorrows of my Soul

    I AM Mother of God

    Oh be unto me, Thy favor Blessed

    I AM Mother of God.

Yes, Mary received her Child

    Yes, Mary received her Child

    She knew the sorrows of her Soul

    She bent the reed and was blown

    Like the thistle in the wind

    Yes Mary knew the sorrow of the Soul.

She taught us the story of that Love

    That we are more than we know

    Yes Mary taught us

    We her children now as of old

    Yes Mary knows and understands

    That's why she loves us so

Mary knows and understands

    That we are more than we know

    When our hearts are torn

    We her children now as of old

    Embrace the story of that Love

    That's Why She loves us so.

    That's Why We Love Her So.

OBLIVIOUS BEING

My inner space of Being has been infiltrated by outside forces beyond my control.

Balance and harmony have been outwitted by greed and testimony to options that are not conducive to this state of bliss.

Fragmented occurrences intercept wholeness. Fatigue sets in. Frustrations dissipate energies of the Light-being world.

I recollect and administer grace.

Basically relationship to oneself in relation to others.

I want to be with Thee, my ME

How do I orchestrate such endeavor

Of Wholeness – of Being

We are One in Thee. Amen.

Oblivious to my Being I get sidetracked

Distractions insurmountable obstruct the pathway.

How do I balance – respond to these

enfoldments – unfoldments?

Oh God, I beseech Thee to me Me

Oh so little the me. Oh so big the Thee.

Where is recompense?

Where is shelter in the storm?

In the bliss of circumstance

In the bliss of Being

I unfold to be Thee

In the wake of forgetfulness.

Oh be it unto my Soul to worship Thee

How sacred is Thy countenance, Thy being.

Let us hold tight to the forward moving Light

To behold me to be Thee. Amen.

In the stillness of the night I listen

In the moments of unrequited space

You exist and make known your presence to me.

The healed Soul responds

It makes manifest the dreams of yesteryear

The longing heart persists – aches for recognition,
    for presence, for possibility

Yes, it is right and just. It is inevitable

The covenant of God to Man cannot be broker.

The comfort of Thy explicit message

The rapture of Thy holy embrace

Grant shelter in the storm

And perseverance in the race.

Your resurrection embodies our resurrection

To forgiveness, to compassion to all that is

And moves on to embrace the eternal NOW. Amen.

What of catapulted desires

What of eternal bliss

What of essence and being

All that is?

I thwart not the path

I remain faithful to thee, my little one

Over and above manifestations of deliverance

To light, to love, to being, to glory

In Resurrection and Ascension to the

Father, through the Father, with the Father

in the Father. Amen.

POETIC MEDITATION

In my countless abode of grace

I behold Thee in me.

Oh sacred the path to whole being.

In the riches and wealth of yesteryear

I am now the emanation of Thy goodness and rapture

The spring of violets and yellow dandelion

Beckon me to creative harmony with Mother Earth

Sacred and precious are your bowels in the darkest depth.

We let go in humility and accept the glories of
    compassion and forgiveness within the little me.

In our wanderings in lost abrasions of fathomless depth

We come to our sense of magnanimity

Magnificence in being the Resurrected Lamb of God

Eros of God who takes away the sin of the World

We join Jesus in the human-divine nature

    to recreate the world.

And become that divine manifestation of the Christ

To transform the world – be become becoming

The true soul the authentic soul of God.

Matter transformed in love and light feminine and masculine

The Cosmic Christ indeed is with us here and now

Always and ever to awaken our deep wishes of the heart

To express and be the Soul of God

Our rightful heritage in the covenant of God with Us.

RESENTMENTS, OVERWORK, LACK OF PLAY

I have so much to do today

And yet I await the divine call

To be me

My soul sorrows at lost energy and time.

Obligations before me take up my energy

The child cries

The child needs food

The child needs grace

The child needs love

The child is like the dandelion blown in the wind and scattered

The child needs guidance

The child needs mentoring

The child is lost and needs to be found to get on track on purpose

Resentments, overwork and lack of play distort the picture
Imbalance brings lack of harmony.
My soul cries.

Help O Lord! Help Guardian angel! Help Brotherhood!
Help Sisterhood of God.
My life has been difficult and in torment.
I need a new vision to see and respond boldly,
To the claims of the kingdom.

The energy of money distorts the real energy of ME!
I have resentments founded or unfounded.
Let my life proceed in compassion
And forgiveness of all outside me as well
As within myself.

My own soul needs attention
Over-extension of my physical body
Leaves me at whim's fancy.
Danger sets in,
Grant help to change this predicament.
Amen. Alleluia. Thanks to be God.

I seek balance in my life.

ME (version 2)

My ME is invisible

My ME is mysterious

My ME is foreboding

My ME is God

How do I reconcile differences-imbalances?

My me is resentful, unforgiving, obstinate.

Why is this harmony so difficult to orchestrate?

In Oneness, in Being, in Action, in Love?

Opposite forces are at work.

Will I always live in conflict?

How can I balance and bring together

The Harmony I desire?

In the recesses of the heart, compassion exists

Compassion for the little me, oh so little.

In the tomb of deliverance

In the stretches of the imagination, the divine erupts.

The poor soul acknowledges defeat.

Honor and glory put aside, I exist.

I AM ME.

AUTHENTICITY

I need to live authentically

    Be Love Do

To live authentically, we must live out the process

    Be Love Do

Be – following the divine guidance within.

Love – living, being, doing from the heart in the moment.

Do – action – carrying out the being and loving in act and will.

I boldly come forth to explore the depths of my being. The tensions within my soul arise in juxtaposition to balance the me. Outside forces give vent to explosive frustrations.

REMEMBRANCE – LETTING GO

The laughter, the love, the pain, the Suffering. My soul rejoices; my soul cries; my soul grieves. The Beauty of Thy forgiveness heals and bridges the gap of misunderstandings, missed communication. But Thy Love endures forever.

Oh my Soul – respond. End the struggle! The fight, the conflict with myself. Harmony is here in the midst of grief. I endure, forever.

The immortal Beingness confirms to simplicity of Being. Respond in the moment. The healing touch envelops All of me/ME. That me who fights, retreats, records – oblivious to my Being.

Come forth, oh child anew. It is time. Let go. Be ME in fullness of I. You are the Gem eternal. The Spirits' Guide and Embellishment to be the New Man-Woman on Earth as in Heaven. How lovely Thy sight, Thy Beauty beyond the dreams of We.

Are not the tempest and the sword stilled? Yes, to receive Thy/My will be done on Earth as it is in Heaven! The resistant soul is swayed by Thy enormity to be Who and What I AM: Son/Daughter of God.

My Soul cries and mourns. Yes! It is time. the Spirit has wooed Thee in adornment, in grace, in Love. You are the GEM, the Mystery unfolded. Yes to be who and what We are. Truly – Sons and Daughters of God. Thanks be to God, Amen.

It is time to move to new ground. The Soul is so vulnerable, so sensitive. It is a victim of attachment, sensible or not. The mystery unfolds to teach me/us. It is time. The grief stricken heart lets go to receive Thee in the fullness of Who I AM.

The Beauty of the Soul so misunderstood now comes to terms with Thy/My Being. The fight, the struggle is ended. I AM ME. Son/Daughter of God. God in expression. The Journey of the Soul is unveiled and shared in experience of understanding. Amen! So be it! Alleluia. Thanks be to GOD!

The clinging vine resist temptation to be what I AM – Son of God. It is time to release old patterns and manifest the true SELF. And show the colors of authenticity. Let go and be ME!

"DIVINE IS THE MEDIATRIX OF DEPENDENT ARISING"[2]

This evidence precludes any substance not conducive to the honorable well-being and sacred calling of man/woman to be what he/she is – Sons and Daughters of God. This means living, being, doing from the authentic Self. The destiny of man is to be – live – do in concretized form the fullest expression of God on/in Earth! What a momentous calling. No wonder angels were envious of MAN/WOMAN!

---

[2] Benedictine Monk quoting Bede Griffiths on Radio PBD New Dimension Program 28-38.

But the price is real. Much adversity is to be overcome – abandoned. Radical change is inevitable. Dedicated giving of the Self to the world in service is part and parcel of this journey.

We have a calling bigger than ourselves. May we be blessed with circumstances conducive to this WORK. Amen! Thanks be to God. Amen. So be it. Alleluia.

NOSTALGIA

In the wake of circumstance

I look at what is before me

I go down the narrow hallway

A light shines through

There in the abode of grace

My heart swells in magnitude

Forgiveness and compassion lead our Souls

in a new realm, a realm of GRACE.

The Heart loves – feels – speaks the WISDOM

of ages past and those to come.

How poor my/our spirit

I beckon YOU to come

Uplift me/us to be who I/WE AM/ARE

Glorious in Mission.

I-WE give thanks. Amen. Alleluia.

> In the wake of circumstance I look at what is before me.
>
> I go down the narrow hallway.
>
> A light shines through
>
> There in the abode of grace, my heart swells in magnitude.

THE AWAKENING CALL TO LIFE

In the mystery of my Being one in Thee I come to the awakening call of justice – foreboding grace.

In my destiny of becoming, I probe the mystery of life: the ancients call to justice, the clamor of evil, notwithstanding to envelop all.

My beneficent deliverance to Life has rescued me from the torments of my Soul. Fear and Guilt, obstacles to my becoming are shed like mud in a drenching rain to relive the burden of defeat.

Repentance, forgiveness, mercy transform us to be who we are meant to be in the awakening call to Life through God with God, in God. Amen. So be it. Alleluia.

With a thankful heart, peace to my Soul, joy in abundance, I proceed to be God in expression, here and now in my earthly experience. Amen. Thanks be to God.

MY INNER CHILD, THE DIVINE WITHIN

Speak to me, Christ child.

I have been too long in oblivious being.

Awaken in me the portals of grace.

My distressed body, mind and spirit

    paid its toll in resentments, anger,

frustration, on-going conflicts with clutter,

and family agendas.

I seek to have some respite from the demands, the obligations
that interfere with be – become – becoming.

Open my heart to forgive, let go, release

all the baggage that interferes with your

generous abode of GRACE. I ask to receive

and knock so the door will open wide.

Let my frustrated, saddened broken heart

Be lifted out of the mud and mire

To express who and what I AM – Child of God!

My inner child speaks!

1) Express gratitude for <u>all</u> blessings – opportunities, challenges, everything.
2) Become decisive – focused – single minded.
3) Grow in the spirit in community.
4) Write and publish. Share gifts in the world.
5) Be a light in the world.
6) Honor the sacred in evil to be transformed in the world.
7) Abide in grace.

Open the portals to grace.

The longing heart persists.

Perseverance unlimited

In the abode of grace.

Be it unto my Soul, Oh Lord God

Heaven and Earth meet to transform

Thee to be ME. Amen.

THE TERRORISTS

May their Souls be likened to a Ship

The rudder steadfast.

To bring justice through love, compassion

And Grace through us, with us and in us.

Amen. Thanks be to God. Alleluia.

Out of the depths I am lifted up

In the firmament

Blessed be my Soul

Blessed be Me – You – I – Us – It

Thanks be to God! Amen.

SURRENDER

Step back – let it occur on its own. Let go of my ideas.

Mother – Her Divine Light – Feminine Compassionate Nature of God New World

You know the heart of ME NOW. You live the seed of ME now.

The Act of Intimacy in culture

Be it unto my soul to forgive the obstacles

never ending. Let grace abide in me every moment.

CONFESSION

Confession in its truest sense is the ongoing expression in the heart of forgiveness to all for all in all by the recipient of grace. It is an act of the will to respond to the ever-present grace of God, the universe, notwithstanding. Ordinarily, the focus is on immediate circumstances, and interaction with the person or people in one's daily life. It includes the primary act of forgiving oneself in receiving God's forgiveness as well as forgiving God!

COMMUNION

Behold the Con of ME. Communion is that quiet receptivity of the soul to enter into dialogue with the grace of God. It is essentially a receiving of the Divine essence imparted to the uniqueness of the individual soul. This act of grace can take a variety of forms in the co-creative act of humanity with God. It pervades all the fields of study by humans. Our great literature, art, music, science all partake of this wondrous activity. All modes of activity that enhance the life of humanity come from this divine embrace. The greatest example of this embrace can be found in the lives of the Holy Family: Jesus, Mary and Joseph. Compassion, Love.

AM I A STRANGER TO MYSELF?

Yes, in giving. Who and what do I give and support?

It is not I. This creates resentment and one constantly is forgiving (in need). Instead of releasing the baggage and developing and being ME!

What does this entail? Change. What kind of change? I do not know. Help me God on this intricate path at home and in the world.

Amen. So be it. Thanks be to God!

I'm waiting for an answer. Help!

THE THREE POWERS OF DEATH

The Soul. The Heart. The Mind.

In the fullness of the spiritual journey the soul dies a certain death. The soul benefits from the continual pruning of old embedded patterns of thought, word and deed. It is a lengthy process in which the will succumbs to the blessings of truth. The Soul is moved by grace to respond in keeping with the unique destiny it is meant to fulfill. Constant vigilance is the path in this divine embrace guided by faith and trust.

The hardened heart moves slowly into clear water. the fears, guilt, anger, resentment, hate, envy, unforgiveness etc. are slowly released and replaced with a calm acceptance and state of evenness. Humility, compassion are attributes of this state in recognizing oneness and interdependence of all.

The mind no longer plays tricks in the imagination. Wisdom, love, harmony and peace are the motivating forces directing one's life and interactions with oneself and others. The harmonious union and balancing and reconciliation of opposites play out in the actions, thoughts and words of each of us in the world.

GRACE

Grace is the unequivocal demeanor of bliss. This means we are in a state of shock and absurdity in the unfolding and random performances in everyday life until we reach that point of realized knowing who and what we are: children of God, agents of God to perform and exhibit those divine qualities that propel us into realized conscious existence – LIFE!

The degrees of grace are commensurate with our innate gifts of unfolding: the openness of heart, mind and soul to respond in any given moment. This explains the "Power of NOW," the instant we are one with our Creator.

As Co-creator, we spontaneously respond to the integral action of bliss: the process of expressing our intrinsic self and demeanor. Clarity and decision awaken the dormant gem in each and every one of us.

HARD WORK DOES NOT GET US TO HEAVEN.

It takes consciousness

Thought. Word. Deed.

Rest Yes Rest!

A Moment Alone!

Solitude: Not mine – But Thine!

When we tap into that deep reservoir of our unique self, we become a new person.

It is difficult to meet expectations in the immediate and extended family as well as our endeared community of worship and fellowship.

Sometimes, we are alone only with our God. Our soul feels adrift and saddened by this expulsion from a different paradise of our ancestry of coming to a new consciousness.

How can I disconnect with my other human beings and remain true to the human suffering experience?

Impossible!

CLUTTER

Take little steps.
Arrive at solutions.
Be an angel of light.
Blow into the circle of events and
    shatter the wellspring of existence
    into meaningful wholes.
Be a light to your soul.
Throw off the meaningless into the fire.

Be it unto my Soul to forgive the
    abomination of circumstance.

Mary, Queen of Heaven and Earth,
    Pray for us.
Thank You!

HUMILITY

True Humility is that ingredient, disposition of the soul in the awakened heart that corresponds in relationship of Thy/My will as One and the same in all through all, with all. It honors the self in obligatory fashion. It searches for the light in one's soul to become the best one can be. The unique God given gifts we are given are discovered, explored and developed to share in the world:

This awesome world of endless variety for all, with all, in all, through all constantly challenges us to stay the course. Thy/My will be done.

Amen. Thanks be to God.

COMPASSION

I contemplate the soul in Me. Let it rest in peace and stillness. Ever forthcoming in soul's delights. Misfortunes anticipated dissipated through the divine embodiment of Jesus in the soul. Eros awakened electrified in magnifying the divine attributes in the Earth experience, body, heart, mind, soul, spirit. Amen. Alleluia. Thanks be to God.

Compassion, empathy, being at one with all humans, all earth creatures, all rock, plant, mineral, animal! All that is. Amen.

Let the heavens reap the Joy in Spirit and send this Joy to the deepest and darkest elements of existence. Amen. Thanks be to God. Alleluia.

May your bounty be reaped by the masses in conscious awakening to the riches of the Kingdom. Amen.

Thanks be to God.
Alleluia.

THE LAST GIFT – NEW LIFE

    The Tree of Life

    Unspoiled by furls of anger and power

    Offsets the seasons of the time.

    The Tree of Life re-echoes Love's reward.

    The rarest gift of all –

    Unspoken, Unheard, Understood,

    Spirit, Heart, Soul joined and reconciled

    Destiny fulfilled and tearing open

    The Curtain of dawn. New Life!

About the Author
Kathleen David

Kathleen David was born in Frankenstein, Missouri. She moved to Athens, Georgia in 1964 where she still resides. She has dedicated her life to her family, masterful cooking, creating beautiful spaces, and writing. Through her writing, she seeks to find wholeness and hopes that others will be encouraged to take their unique journeys in fulfilling their purpose in life. Kathleen loves to take walks, enjoy nature, swim, and socialize in her spare time.

www.ingramcontent.com/pod-product-compliance
Lightning Source LLC
Chambersburg PA
CBHW070722240426
43673CB00003B/111